33 DAYS

33 DAYS

LÉON WERTH (1878–1955) was born in Remiremont, France, to a Jewish clothier. Though he was a brilliant student, he dropped out of school to devote himself to writing art criticism, publishing his first critique in the *Paris-Journal* in 1911. His first novel, *The White House*, was a finalist for the Prix Goncourt in 1913. Werth was an anti-bourgeois anarchist, a bohemian, and a leftist Bolshevik supporter. In spite of his politics, however, he was assigned to be a radio operator during World War I, until he was diagnosed with a lung infection and released from service. In 1922, he married Suzanne Canard, and she would later also become active in the Resistance. Werth wrote critically of the Nazi movement and colonialism, became a Gaullist, and contributed to Claude Mauriac's journal *Liberté de l'Esprit*. In 1931, he was introduced to Antoine de Saint-Exupéry by a mutual friend, and they become extremely close. Saint-Exupéry referred to Werth in three of his books and dedicated two to him. In addition to *33 Days*, Werth also wrote *Déposition*, his journals from 1940 to 1944, while hiding from the Nazis in the Jura Mountains region. He died in Paris on December 13, 1955, at the age of seventy-seven.

ANTOINE DE SAINT-EXUPÉRY (1900–1944) was a poet, philosopher, aviator, and the author of *The Little Prince*, which has been translated into over 250 languages. His interest in flying inspired him to write *Wind, Sand and Stars* and *Night Flight*. He disappeared over the Mediterranean during a military reconnaissance mission in July 1944.

AUSTIN DENIS JOHNSTON, a former editor, spent seventeen years at Time, Inc., where he also supervised French and Spanish translations.

THE NEVERSINK LIBRARY

I was by no means the only reader of books on board the Neversink. *Several other sailors were diligent readers, though their studies did not lie in the way of belles-lettres. Their favourite authors were such as you may find at the book-stalls around Fulton Market; they were slightly physiological in their nature. My book experiences on board of the frigate proved an example of a fact which every book-lover must have experienced before me, namely, that though public libraries have an imposing air, and doubtless contain invaluable volumes, yet, somehow, the books that prove most agreeable, grateful, and companionable, are those we pick up by chance here and there; those which seem put into our hands by Providence; those which pretend to little, but abound in much.* —HERMAN MELVILLE, *WHITE JACKET*

33 DAYS

LÉON WERTH

WITH AN INTRODUCTION BY
ANTOINE DE SAINT-EXUPÉRY

TRANSLATED BY AUSTIN DENIS JOHNSTON

MELVILLE HOUSE PUBLISHING
BROOKLYN · LONDON

33 DAYS

Originally published by Viviane Hamy, 1992
Copyright © 1992 by Léon Werth
Translation copyright © 2015 by Austin Denis Johnston
"Lettre à l'ami" copyright © by Antoine de Saint-Exupéry

First Melville House printing: April 2015

Grateful acknowledgment is made to the Estate of
Antoine de Saint-Exupéry for permission to print "Letter to a Friend."

Melville House Publishing		8 Blackstock Mews
145 Plymouth Street	and	Islington
Brooklyn, NY 11201		London N4 2BT

mhpbooks.com   facebook.com/mhpbooks   @melvillehouse

Library of Congress Cataloging-in-Publication Data
Werth, Léon, 1878–1955.
 [33 jours. English]
 33 days : a memoir / Léon Werth ; translated by Austin Denis
Johnston ; with ["Letter to a Friend"] by Antoine de Saint-Exupéry.
  pages   cm. — (Neversink)
 ISBN 978-1-61219-425-7 (paperback)
 ISBN 978-1-61219-426-4 (ebook)
 1. Werth, Léon, 1878–1955. 2. Authors, French—20th century—
Biography. 3. World War, 1939–1945—Personal narratives, French.
4. World War, 1939–1945—France. I. Saint-Exupéry, Antoine de,
1900–1944. II. Title.

PQ2645.E7A1813 2015
848.91209—dc23
 [B]
                                        2015002131

Design by Christopher King

Cover photograph: Exodus, Place de Rome, Paris, June 12–13, 1940.
Courtesy of © Roger-Viollet / The Image Works

Printed in the United States of America
10 9 8 7 6 5 4 3 2 1

Cet ouvrage publié dans le cadre du programme d'aide
à la publication bénéficie du soutien du Ministère des Affaires Étrangères et
du Service Culturel de l'Ambassade de France représenté aux États-Unis.

This work, published as part of a program of aid for publication, received
support from the French Ministry of Foreign Affairs and the
Cultural Service of the French Embassy in the United States.

Cet ouvrage a bénéficié du soutien des Programmes d'aide à la
publication de l'Institut Français.

This work, published as part of a program of aid for publication,
received support from the Institut Français.

CONTENTS

EDITOR'S NOTE

This book is based on a manuscript that was smuggled out of Nazi-occupied France in October 1940 by Antoine de Saint-Exupéry, who took it to New York with the intent of getting the book published in English. But the manuscript—which consisted of his friend Léon Werth's firsthand account of his escape just months before from Paris, and an introduction to that account written by Saint-Exupéry himself—was never published, and subsequently vanished. Fifty years later, in 1992, Werth's French-language text was rediscovered and published by the French publisher Viviane Hamy. However, that edition did not include Saint-Exupéry's introduction, which remained lost. In 2014, the introduction was rediscovered in a Canadian library by Melville House, and thus this book represents not only the first English-language edition of *33 Days*, but the first edition to include both the complete, original text and the introduction, as originally intended by Werth and Saint-Exupéry.

Werth had asked Saint-Exupéry to smuggle the book out of France because, as a Jew, Werth was not allowed by the French government to publish anything. Forced to hide out in France's Jura Mountains and unable to move about as easily as his non-Jewish friend, Werth also no doubt felt, as did Saint-Exupéry, that an English-language version of his gripping, firsthand testimony might be useful to Saint-Exupéry in his greater mission in going to New York, which was to stir American support for intervention. After all, the story of the massive French flight from the approaching Nazi *Werhmacht* in May and June of 1940—a migration of such biblical proportions as to now be called by historians "*l'Exode*," or "The Exodus"—was largely unknown in the United States. Werth's account remains, in fact, one of the few eyewitness documentations of the Exodus, which is estimated to have involved more than eight million people, and to have been the largest mass migration in human history.

In New York, Saint-Exupéry did manage to find an agreeable publisher: Brentano's, a bookstore that during the war years also published French-language books in translation. Saint-Exupéry asked for nothing more than a military parcel consisting of chocolate, cigarettes, and water purification tablets for payment, and was so certain of the publication that he mentioned *33 Days* in a book of his own published around that time, *Pilote de guerre*. However, for reasons that remain unknown, the book never appeared, and the manuscript was lost. Saint-Exupéry was apparently so frustrated by the failed publication that he took his introduction, at least, and expanded it into another wartime book, *Letter to a Hostage*, with the "hostage" being Werth—who goes unnamed for his protection.

While Werth would survive the war and go on to write numerous books, Saint-Exupéry would not: his plane disappeared while on a reconnaissance mission over the Mediterranean in July 1944, presumably shot down by the Germans.

But *33 Days*, in addition to being a vivid and harrowing first-person account of one of modern history's major events, and a welcome introduction in English to an important French writer, stands as a testament to a long-term friendship tempered in wartime, that of Léon Werth and Antoine de Saint-Exupéry—who dedicated his most famous work, *The Little Prince*, to Werth:

> I ask children to forgive me for dedicating this book to a grown-up. I have a serious excuse: this grown-up is the best friend I have in the world . . . He lives in France, where he is hungry and cold. He needs to be comforted.

INTRODUCTION:
LETTER TO A FRIEND

BY ANTOINE DE SAINT-EXUPÉRY

I.

In December 1940, when I passed through Portugal to go to the United States, Lisbon seemed like a kind of bright, sad haven to me. At the time there was a lot of talk about an imminent invasion. Portugal clung to an appearance of happiness. Lisbon, which had built the most beautiful international exposition in the world, was smiling a weak smile, like that of mothers who've had no news of a son at the front and are trying to protect him with their confidence: "My son is alive because I smile . . ." The same way Lisbon was saying, "Look how happy and peaceful and brightly lit I am . . ." The entire continent loomed over Portugal like a mountain wilderness, swarming with its packs of hunters. A festive Lisbon defied Europe: "Can I be a target when I make such a point of not hiding! When I'm so vulnerable! When I'm so happy . . ."

At night my country's cities were the color of ashes. I'd weaned myself off all light, and this radiant capital gave me a strange uneasiness. If the surrounding neighborhood is dark, the diamonds in a too-brightly lit store window attract prowlers. We feel them circling. I feel Europe's night, inhabited by shadowy monsters, looming over Lisbon. Perhaps wandering groups of bombers were sniffing at this treasure.

But Portugal ignored the monster's looming. Ignored it with all its might. Portugal was talking about art with an almost desperate confidence. Would anyone dare destroy it amid its cult of art? It had brought out all its treasures. Would anyone dare destroy it amid its treasures? It showed off its great men. For lack of an army, for lack of cannons, it had marshaled its stone guards—the poets, the explorers, the conquistadors—against the invader's iron. For lack of an army and cannons, Portugal's entire past barred the way. Would anyone dare destroy it amid its legacy of a grandiose past?

So every evening I wandered sadly through the triumphs of this exposition of supreme taste, where everything approached perfection, even the music, so discreet, chosen with such delicacy, that flowed gently over the gardens, quietly, like the simple melody of a fountain. Was anyone going to eradicate this marvelous sense of proportion from the world?

And I found Lisbon, with its desperate smile, sadder than my darkened cities.

I've known, maybe you have too, those slightly bizarre families that reserved the place at their table of someone who had died. They refused to let death in. But I didn't see any consolation in that. The dead should be dead. Then, in their role as dead, they find a different kind of presence. But these families postponed their return. They changed them into eternal absentees, into friends late for eternity. They traded mourning for a meaningless waiting. And to me these households seemed plunged into an unremitting malaise that was sad in a way different than sorrow. Guillaumet, the last friend I lost, who was shot down flying mail service into Syria, I count him as dead, by God. He'll never change. He'll never be here again, but he'll never be absent either. I removed his place setting from my table— a useless trap that didn't snare him—and I made him a truly dead friend.

But Portugal was trying to believe in happiness, keeping its place—and its Chinese lanterns and its music—at the table. In Lisbon they played desperately at being happy so that God might be willing to believe it.

But, above all, the ones who made Lisbon so sad were certain refugees, not the outcasts in search of some temporary safety, but those who were repudiating the misery of theirs to become expatriates forever.

Unable to find accommodations in the city itself, I was staying in Estoril, near the casino. I survived intense warfare, given that my group, which had flown missions over Germany nonstop for nine months, had lost three-quarters of its crews in the lone German offensive. Returning home, I'd experienced the grim atmosphere of slavery and the threat of famine. I had lived through the pitch-black night of our cities. And here, just steps from my place, every evening the casino in Estoril was filled with ghosts. Noiseless Cadillacs, with the pretense of going somewhere, deposited them on the fine sand at the main entrance. They had dressed, old style, for dinner. They showed off their ascots or their pearls. They had invited one another to the bit players' dinner, where they had nothing to say to each other.

Then, depending on their wealth, they played roulette or baccarat. Sometimes I went to watch them. I felt neither indignation nor irony, but a vague anxiety. What disturbs you at the zoo facing the survivors of an extinct species. They set themselves up around the tables. They squeezed against a stern croupier, trying to feel hope, fear, despair, envy and jubilation. Like the living. They gambled fortunes that perhaps, at that very moment, had become meaningless. They used currencies that, perhaps, were discontinued. Perhaps the securities in their safes were guaranteed by factories already confiscated or, threatened as they were by aerial bombing, already being destroyed. They were drawing funds from Sirius. In resuming the past, they were trying to believe in the legitimacy of their excitement, the validity of their checks, the perpetuity of their contracts, as if nothing on earth had begun to collapse several months ago. It was unreal. It was a dolls' ballet. But it was sad.

No doubt they felt nothing. I left them. I went for a breath of air along the shore. And the sea at Estoril, at this resort town, this domesticated sea, also seemed part of the game. It pushed a single, feeble wave, glistening brightly with moonlight, into the bay, like an inappropriate ball gown.

I met my refugees again on the ship. The atmosphere on this ship also exuded a mild anxiety. The ship was transferring, from one continent to another, those who had been called back to life. I thought: "I'd gladly be a traveler; I don't want to be an emigrant. I learned a lot of things when I was young. I want to use them." But here are my refugees pulling little address books from their pockets. The remnants of their identities. They were still pretending to be someone. They were clinging with all their might to some meaning. "You know, I'm so-and-so . . . ," they said, ". . . from such-and-such city . . . the friend of so-and-so . . . Do you know so-and-so?"

And they told you the story of some friend, or some position, or some misdeed, or any other story that could connect them to anyone. But, because they were expatriating, none of this past was going to be of use to them any longer. It was still very warm, very fresh, very alive, like the memories of a love affair are at first. You make a bundle of letters, tie them together with great care. You add a few souvenirs. And, initially, the bundle develops a melancholy charm. Then a blonde with blue eyes walks by, and the bundle dies. Because the friend, the position, the hometown, the memories of the house fade too when they're no longer useful . . .

They felt that keenly. Just as Lisbon pretended to be happy, they pretended to believe they were going to return soon. The prodigal son's absence is easy: it's a false absence because, behind him, his home remains. Whether someone is absent in the next room or on the other side of the planet isn't important. The presence of someone apparently far away can become more substantial than before he left. That's what happens in prayers. I never loved my home more than in the Sahara. Never was a woman more present to others than the fiancées of sixteenth-century Breton sailors rounding Cape Horn and weakening against the wall of headwinds. From departure, they already began coming home. It's their return they were preparing when hoisting the sails with their thick hands. The shortest route from the port in Brittany to their fiancée's house went through Cape Horn. But here my refugees seemed like Breton sailors whose fiancées had been taken from them. No Breton fiancée lit a humble lamp in her window for them anymore. They weren't prodigal sons. They were prodigal sons without a home. That's when the real journey outside oneself begins.

How to reconstruct yourself? How to remake the dense fabric of memories inside yourself? So this ghost ship was full, like limbo, of souls to be born. The only ones who seemed real, so real we'd have liked to touch them with a finger, were those who were part of the ship and, dignified by real functions, carried platters, dried pans, polished shoes. And, with a certain contempt, served the dead. It's not poverty that earned the refugees the crew's mild disdain. It's not money they lacked, but substance. They were no longer the man of such-and-such a household, with such-and-such a friend, such-and-such a position. They pretended to be, but it was no longer true. No one needed them, no one was going to ask them for help. How wonderful that telegram is that upsets you, gets you up in the middle of the night, sends you to the train station: "Hurry! I need you!" Friendships are made quickly with those who help you. They're made deliberately with those who ask to be helped. Certainly, no one hated my ghosts, no one envied them, no one importuned them, but no one loved them with the only love that mattered. I thought: they'll be busy from the moment they arrive with welcome cocktails, consolation dinners; they'll get the most helpful reception from a generous America. There one can knock on any door, ask and receive. But who will knock on theirs asking to be taken in? "Open up! It's me!" A child must breastfeed a long time before he demands. A friend must be cultivated a long time before he claims friendship's due. Generations must ruin themselves repairing a crumbling old château to learn to love it.

II.

So I was thinking: "The main thing is that what we have experienced resides somewhere. So do the customs. And the family celebrations. And the house with memories. And so on . . . What's most important is to live for the return." And I felt threatened to my very core by the fragility of those distant poles on which I depended. I risked experiencing a true desert and began to understand a mystery that had long puzzled me.

I spent three years in the Sahara. Like so many others, I fanta-
sized about its strange powers. Whoever has experienced life in the
Sahara, where everything appears to be nothing but solitude and
destitution, nonetheless mourns those years as the most beautiful
they've lived. The phrases "nostalgia for the sand, nostalgia for the
solitude, nostalgia for the space" are nothing but literary formulas,
and they explain nothing. Yet it's here, aboard this ship teeming with
passengers piled on top of each other, that for the first time I felt
as if I understood the desert. Certainly, the Sahara offers nothing
but flat sand, or more precisely gravel, as far as the eye can see, for
dunes there are rare. There, nothing visible is moving. There, you are
separated from everything you love. You wallow endlessly in the atmosphere of boredom. And yet invisible divinities are there building
a network of routes, gradients and signs, a secret, living musculature.
Uniformity doesn't exist. Everything is oriented. Even a silence there
doesn't resemble another silence.

There is a silence of peace, when the tribes are reconciled, when
the evening cool returns and it seems as if you were putting in, sails
furled, at a quiet harbor. There's a silence at noon, when the sun sus-
pends all thought and movement. There's a false silence when the
north wind flags and insects appear, ripped away from oases in the
interior like pollen, presaging a sandstorm from the east. There's a
silence of brewing plots, when you know that some distant tribe is
simmering. There's a mysterious silence when the Arabs gather for
their indecipherable confabulations. There's a tense silence when a
messenger is late returning. An acute silence when, at night, you
hold your breath to listen. A melancholy silence if you're remembering someone you love.

Everything has its focus. Each star sets a true course. They are all
stars of the magi. They all serve their god. One points the way to a
far-off well, hard to reach. And the distance that separates you from
the well looms like a castle wall. One points the way to a dry well.
And the star itself seems dry. And the distance that separates you
from the empty well is all uphill. Some other star serves as a guide to
an unknown oasis that nomads have rhapsodized about, but which
rebellion makes off-limits to you. And the sand that separates you

and the oasis is a field of fairy tales. One points the way to a bustling city in the south, delightful as sinking your teeth into fruit. One, the way to the sea.

Still-more-distant poles magnetize this desert: a house in France that remains a vivid memory. A potluck long ago with comrades. A friend you know nothing about except that he exists.

Thus you feel fraught or invigorated by force fields that draw or repel you, that you approach or resist. You are well-based, well-oriented, well-positioned at the center of the cardinal directions.

And since the desert offers no tangible splendor, since there is nothing to see or hear in the desert, you are forced to recognize that, far from being lulled to sleep, your inner life grows stronger and that man is animated above all by invisible structures. Man is ruled by spirit. In the desert, I'm worth what my deities are.

Whether in the Sahara or not, space is always animated for us by vital currents. Just as in the desert if I have the feeling of distance, it's the influence of a far-off well, and if in the mountains I have the sensation of an abyss, it's gravity pulling me downward, so if I'm rich in magnetic poles aboard this depressing ship, it's thanks to Léon Werth's house, among others. For Léon Werth is my friend.

France is not an abstract deity. France is not a history textbook. France is not some ideology. France is the flesh that sustains me, a network of connections that rules me, a collection of axes that are the foundation of my affections. That's why I need those to whom I'm attached to outlast me. To be oriented, I need them to exist. Otherwise, how would I know where or what to return to? That's why, Léon Werth, during my crossing I so needed to reassure myself of your presence in that house in the Jura that I knew so well, so that one of the cardinal points of my world would be preserved. Only then, while wandering distantly in the empire of your friendship, which has no boundaries, could I feel like a traveler and not an emigrant. For the desert isn't where we think it is. The Sahara is livelier than a capital, and the most crowded of cities becomes a desert if the essential poles of life are demagnetized.

33 DAYS

AUTHOR'S PREFACE

It was the time when they were "correct," which preceded the time when they gave us "lessons in politeness."

I

FROM PARIS TO CHAPELON. THE CARAVAN

On June 10th, at eleven o'clock in the morning, I meet Tr. on the Avenue des Champs-Élysées. We decide to go as far as the Hotel Continental "to get some answers." In the middle of the avenue, a laborer with a jackhammer is digging up a few cobblestones. Street repairs or defense against tanks? Meanwhile, a sprinkler spreads pearls of water over the turf of a lawn. This sprinkler makes us think childish thoughts, it gives us confidence: "If things were that serious, they wouldn't think of watering the grass . . ."

"Godspeed," I say to him while leaving. "In wartime," he tells me, "God exists . . ." This is not an expression of faith. He means to say that neither he nor I have any power over events, that history is being made without us.

Rue d'Assas, my street, is empty. The usual motorists, those who park their cars on the sidewalk while they have lunch, left long ago. I'm in no hurry to leave. The wisest, most competent advice has not persuaded me. This is not a matter of reason. My certainty and security are rooted in a deep part of me that neither strategic calculation nor reason can reach. "Paris is Paris, and it's impossible that the Germans would get in."

Nevertheless, during the night, A. gave me a friendly, brotherly order to put sixty kilometers between the Germans and us. I decided to obey, but almost out of kindness. I think his friendship is anxious, as mine would be in a similar situation, and that he's at great risk and yet is afraid only for us.

Like every year, we take the road for Saint-Amour, which is our base within the Jura, Bresse and Lower Burgundy. We leave on June 11th at nine o'clock in the morning. We think that without pressing we'll arrive around five o'clock in the afternoon. Still, a strange departure. Paris is covered by a funnel of soot. I never knew what that black cloud was. Smoke from burning reservoirs of gasoline in Rouen? Some means of warfare devised by us? By the Germans?

I leave the war behind me. I say that sincerely. I give myself permission to relax. Since September of last year, I have tried not to lie and not to lie to myself. I accepted the role of Don Diègue. And I believe that civilization is over, for centuries, if soldiers don't, as General Weygand said, hold their ground. Just this week I tried to picture holding on, to put myself in the shoes of a soldier standing fast. I endured this consent to heroism. This enduring alone consoled and reassured me.

Porte d'Italie, Villejuif, Thiais. The traffic is like any weekday. Soon the road is overcrowded, like a Sunday evening. I stop at a gas station. This woman who holds the gas hose overhead with raised arms, I soon have the feeling that there is something else between her and me than the traffic in fuel. She waits for me. Immobile, she holds the hose over her head; she doesn't take a step toward the car's gas tank. Her eyes look into mine. She tells me, "Russia declared war on Germany . . ."

Her eyes fill with tears. Mine too. How distant the arguments about Stalinism and the revolution seem! Russia launches her armies and the Germans, whether in Compiègne or Pontoise, turn home as if nipped at the heels.

A historian may laugh at my gullibility if he likes, but we so badly need news like that! Of course other news had already circulated in Paris, running along the streets, reaching into concierges' lodges, into bistros and into houses through windows. But that news wasn't false, it told of a disaster verified the following day.

And that piece of news, as you can easily understand, I swallowed with some reluctance. I approached a stopped truck. There were three men in the front seat: "Is it true that . . . ? Have you heard that . . . ?"

"Russia . . . ? Yes."

Russia entering the war, I encountered it all along the road, when the overcrowding became a traffic jam, when the cars advanced four rows across, and at nightfall it was waiting for me, it was hiding in a little village, a little backstreet village far from the route of the exodus.

At Plessis-Chenet the road to Fontainebleau is barred to us and we turn toward Pithiviers, or Orléans, I don't recall. But we are stuck in an endless caravan. We are just one link in a chain that stretches slowly along the road at ten, five kilometers an hour . . . At six in the evening, in the village of Auverneaux, we are forty kilometers from Paris. We find a room. Some courageous people who left Paris on bicycles are already there. In front of a radio, a woman is crying: The *Radio-Journal de France* said nothing about Russia.

We leave the following day, June 12th, at four in the morning. We didn't think anyone got up so early. But again we find the caravan. We roll along with the motor strangled in second gear, more often in first, twenty meters at a time. Then there's a stop of six or seven hours, I don't remember. Six or seven hours in the sun. But among the crowd clogging the roadsides, this elongated crowd, this crowd spread out as if by a rolling mill, there is not yet a trace of ill humor, nor even impatience. It gives way, it believes in giving way, to military needs. And gradually the rumor spreads that some munitions trucks are passing on a crossroad up ahead.

As evening falls we stop in Milly. We have gone sixteen kilometers in fifteen hours.

There are many cars stopped in the town square, at rest or broken down. The hotels, the cafés are full, but the crowd isn't anxious. Traffic is being directed. The local commandant has established a little repair shop where an engineering unit, with kindness and good humor, is helping drivers whose cars have broken down. And Monsieur Popot, a mechanic by trade, sure-handedly measures out for us the mixture of petroleum and oil that an old Bugatti needs to lubricate its transmission.

The market is covered by a handsome roof of old tiles. We find refuge in a café that resembles a *guinguette*.* The dining room is vast, like a café in the Klondike from the movies. The mirror, the palm trees, the yellow walls, the brown baseboards, the tables covered with red enamel make up the decor of a fairground decorated for a wild party. A warlike blonde, the owner, is behind the bar, and the waitress, a mischievous brunette full of sharp repartee, dashes around the room. There is no longer anything to be found anywhere for dinner. But we're allowed to bring our can of sardines.

At the other end of the dining room two soldiers are seated facing each other. The table and a bottle of red wine separate them. They are together but not speaking to each other. They are absolutely still in their chairs. They don't look at one another and their gazes are fixed on different points on the floor. They have an air of timelessness about them.

The hotels are full. We sleep and, the following day, have lunch at the home of a grocer, a "cheese tender." We are welcomed at the family table. Two days has been enough to make us feel uprooted; we're already conscious of the value of rest, refuge, hospitality. It's not that of customers; it's not that of lodgers. The grocers resisted when, out of decency, we wanted to double the price they asked.

We resume our place in the caravan, at a snail's pace. The road to Nemours is closed. We try to get to Joigny by way of Château-Landon and Saint-Julien-du-Saut. But we are redirected toward Malesherbes.

The cars are squeezed together as if at a tollgate. Pedestrians overtake them. No engine likes this speed. But a three-liter 1932 Bugatti protests. The water in the radiator boils. We stop, we start again, but each restart becomes a problem. Because this clutch has every virtue except smoothness. I finesse the clutch. After several hours it's exhausting. It's nerve-racking. The gravity of the moment means little. Less so as the gravity of the moment and mechanical worries combine. We are afraid of breaking down.

After we cross the road to Pithiviers, the water in the radiator boils again. The shoulder is wide enough for an automobile. I pull

---

* An open-air restaurant.

out of the caravan. I park on the right. The road runs along a wood. The caravan files past. Old cars have emerged from their caves in the suburbs or a coachworks museum or the camps where the Roma winter. They are mixed in with the powerful ten-horsepower bourgeois cars covered with suitcases and mattresses. This is the kingdom of mattresses. One would think France is the land of mattresses, that a mattress is the Frenchman's most precious possession. In many of the cars old women lie flat, no longer looking at anything outside themselves, and children sleep as if dead. Commercial trucks are filled with luggage and passengers, like emigrants in steerage, sometimes terraced on piles of baggage, sometimes under a tarpaulin and arranged in rows like the audience at a theater. Through the windows we see dogs, cats, caged birds. A monkey is leashed to a radiator.

One car tows a tiny cart in which an old laborer sits, legs dangling. He has brought only a few bundles and a fishing net. But the cart is not attached to the car by a simple rope for temporary towing. It is attached artistically. A system of ropes, spikes and metal cables connects the two vehicles for the long term, uniting their two destinies. These acts of kindness, this readiness to oblige, will have disappeared by tomorrow.

The caravan of cars is overtaken by cyclists, male and female, and by limping pedestrians. Their heads seem pulled toward their feet. Some carry a travel bag; others have one or two suitcases in hand. Imagine how exhausting this walk is with a valise at the end of your arm. Others push baby carriages—loaded with children, bundles or their most important possessions—or the strangest vehicles cobbled together by handymen out of wooden planks and old bicycle wheels. A woman is seated on the lid of a three-wheeled delivery cart, which a man pedals. An old man on a bicycle, alone, is leading his dog on a leash.

The line of cars moves at the speed of a man on foot, a hundred, fifty, five meters at a time. I can't even let myself contemplate this halting river. My reflex as a motorist compels me to scrutinize its droplets. Mechanically, I evaluate the make and horsepower of the automobiles. The caravan moves and creaks like the chain of a well. It has neither beginning nor end. I'm obsessed by this idiotic phrase:

"The horizon is an imaginary line at the intersection of the sky and the infinite line of cars."

A car stops, driven by a young woman. Like a caterpillar, the caravan flows around it. Inside the automobile there is another woman and an old man. The driver leans against the steering wheel, then raises her arms in desperation. Her engine has stalled, her starter is broken and she has no crank handle. "Put it in gear, step on the clutch . . . we'll push you; when you pick up some speed, let out the clutch . . ." She's asleep, she can't understand me, like a sleepwalker; she confuses in gear and out of gear. We push her car again, the motor turns over, the car starts and then falters momentarily on the road.

Enormous two-wheeled peasants' carts from the Seine-et-Oise and Seine-et-Marne are mixed in with the caravan. They are pulled by massive horses, often by two horses harnessed in line. They are loaded with bedding and sacks of grain and fodder. On one of them is a foal with little appreciation for the joys of being on a wagon. It kicks with all four hooves—now the front, now the rear—and starts bucking epileptically. The dogs leashed underneath the carts wag their happy tails even more.

A farm is nearby. Some people are organizing themselves to spend the night there sleeping on straw. They are tired but not panicked. The battle is far behind them, far behind Paris. They make the best of this involuntary picnic, this camping trip. Tomorrow the roads will be clear.

We arrive in Puiseaux at night. We managed twenty-five kilometers today. We find free space in a beet field. We spend the night in the car. Some military convoys pass by on a distant road. The horses' hooves hitting the ground make a sound like raindrops falling on a roof.

At five in the morning my wife goes into town, lines up until eight o'clock in front of a bakery and brings back a pound of bread. Two hundred meters from the beet field there's a fountain. I had forgotten the miracle of water, the miracle of far-sighted municipalities. I can still feel that water running over my hands. I find a pack of tobacco in town. A few minutes later, the tobacco shop will be closed.

Puiseaux has the shape of a breast, of an anthill, at the summit of which there must be a church. I'm sleepy. It seems to me the winding streets climb to the sky. I'm lost. It will take me an hour to get back to my beet field. The streets are filled with refugees, those with cars, those with wheelbarrows, those from the Nord, those from Paris, those from the Seine-et-Marne. It's part of the caravan, of the caravan dismantled. This crowd resembles nothing I know. Near me someone says: "It's the Canebière."* But here one feels a mute anger, an accumulated impatience in the crowd.

In the street a group is gathered in front of a half-open window listening to the radio. I approach. I couldn't possibly remember what news the circumlocutions of *Radio-Journal* were communicating. It had hardly concealed the German advance. I believe that morning I heard a strange "behind Paris," which reminded me of earlier reports of "fighting west of Brussels" that had not yet announced the capture of Brussels. Nonetheless, for the nomads that we had become, the German advance was still only newspaper headlines. They advance, they cross the Somme, the Oise. Even if they cross the Seine, all is not lost. They will be fought on the Loire. We do not lack rivers, and strategy is the science of rivers.

Meanwhile, a captain, a tall young man with the face of a Bedouin, addresses the crowd, urging it to be hopeful and pointing out that our temporary retreat is the fault of the political half of France, of which he is not part.

I enter a café. Refugees, like flies around a packet of sugar, crowd around the proprietor, who half fills the glasses they hold out to him with pale coffee. For the first time I hear the words, uttered by a drowsy woman with a sullen face: "France is betrayed."

We leave the beet field. In the neighboring car an elderly woman meticulously does her blond hair. We try in vain to take the Château-Landon road to reach Auxerre and the Paris-Lyon highway. We are directed toward Montargis. I hear that at Beaumont we can find gasoline. But news about gasoline is like news about the war. Myths circulate, coming from who knows where.

* The main street in Old Marseille.

A platoon of infantrymen is resting in an empty space between two houses. Some are lying down, asleep. Others, standing, indifferently contemplate the caravan disaggregating in the village. I approach. They were at the Somme. I'm expecting some clarity from them, some hope. But before me are only cryptic, resigned soldiers. In them, I am searching for spirit, depth, volition, desire. They're not handing over their secret. They speak like soldiers. They're tired. From them I get only, "Don't worry . . ."

The invisible authority that is worried about neither traffic jams nor bread nor gasoline vigilantly watches over our itinerary. It redirects us toward Corbeil-en-Gâtinais and Lorcy by way of winding local roads. At nightfall, we arrive in the town of Ladon. We've gone about twenty-five kilometers during the day, at one or two kilometers an hour. We can't bear this anymore. I see a signpost at a crossroads: Chapelon, four kilometers. The road is empty. In my memory it appears dark and rural. I abandon, I extricate myself from this caravan that advances in fits and starts. I take the Chapelon road, where at least we'll find some silence and fresh grass to sleep on.

Why confess this search for refuge in the countryside and this concern for comfort? It's anecdotal and uninteresting. But had we not decided on this detour through the hamlet of Chapelon, we would not have encountered the same circumstances or the same people. We would have run fewer risks, or more. We would not have known some things that I'd dare say put us in touch with historical secrets, that revealed to us a few junctures between history and man.

Four kilometers of empty road, of driving at full speed, of being the brain of the car, of feeling it as one feels one's own body, of feeling the car's chassis as an extension of one's own body, of gliding.

In the village square a group of peasants form a tight circle, posed as if for a commemorative monument. I approach. No sign of suspicion, but they are assessing me, judging me. I've tumbled from the moon into a circle of country notables. Everyone looks at me. I must look very Parisian. I'm not rejected; they don't walk away. I'm being sized up. An old man looks at me as innocently as if he were contemplating the horizon. Among this group of faces, I discern one that's livelier, more defined. This must have been what a young Voltaire looked like, which is to say, Voltaire at forty-five. This face shows more curiosity than the others, and more guile. His eyes aren't sizing me up, they return my gaze.

We are the heroes of fewer than three nights without a bed. Down deep, I think a bed is a good thing. But I'm not so stupid. I too am not without guile. I know how to dissimulate when necessary. I ask only for a roof against bad weather and a little straw.

Abel Delaveau (here I'm giving his real name) was our host. I washed myself with water from his well; we shared meals at his table and slept in a bedroom of his house, a real bedroom, in a bed, a real bed. I contemplated with surprising enthusiasm the 1880 clock on the mantel, the framed photographs and the red underside of the eiderdown.

When I was a child I read beautiful stories about hospitality. The guest is sacred for the biblical patriarch, in the Greeks' *Iliad*, in the Bedouins' tents. Abel, Monsieur Abel as he is often called in Chapelon, I had no reason to envy antiquity thanks to you. Hospitality exists in modern times and is even more beautiful because it is not a rite but a gift.

The courtyard of the farm, filled with the setting sun, with calm, with silence, is enormous and enclosed by a wall. The house, the barns, the stable, the cowshed look beautiful together. In the facade of the house a gothic fragment has been preserved, as one might respect a swallows' nest. I was with Abel Delaveau only long enough to say thank you. A few words about the war changed everything. I'll recount the conversation later. At this point in my story I'll leave it. I'll only say that we felt there was a common language between us. We both detested the war beyond just its effects on our relatives and our interests; we both faced it with surprising acceptance and both knew that if Hitler was responsible, he wasn't as important as he was made out to be and he hadn't invented himself without help.

I've often been uncomfortable chatting with laborers, never with a peasant. Sometimes a peasant picks words with his fingertips, like picking a stalk of wheat, or a single kernel. A city dweller learns from peasants to recognize wheat and oats but can't discuss cereals. A worker learns from newspapers and city life the game of passionate abstractions, of juggling fake weights. When in a crowd, he can't make out the reality, the abstraction and the emotion he's being in-oculated with.

Simply put, Abel Delaveau had read. A government official, as I'll describe him for simplicity's sake, asked me, "Are you sure he as-similated what he had read?" and his question was quick and sharp, as if my assertion had infringed on something at the core of his be-ing. Many French baccalaureates consider this sort of "assimilating" one of their privileges. I knew university faculty members who had assimilated nothing at all.

I thought for a moment about Émile Guillaumin,* to whose home the writer Valery Larbaud brought me one day. But I did not have time to get to know Guillaumin the peasant. I can still see him stabling a cow. The same modesty that kept us from giving in to a conversational *tour littéraire* perhaps kept him from giving a *tour paysan*. But Abel Delaveau was a peasant in full, by heritage and by choice, and an enthusiastic one. I've never met another like him. Especially because he is not at all immured by his work on the land.

That first evening in Chapelon I didn't know that "return to the soil" would soon become a fashionable, prescriptive refrain. Bureau-crats and academics now utter it regularly, proving only that they have no aptitude for anything besides unskilled manual labor. What they call "the wisdom of peasants" is nothing but a reflection of their mental laziness or their preconceptions. They contrast it with work-ers' excitability and are thus reassured. To tell the truth, Abel would not have satisfied them. Still, he would not have been a peasant if he had accepted revolutionary doctrine. But I don't want to do a political portrait of Abel; I don't even know whether I could pull it off. For now it's enough for me to say I never knew a more agile, engaged mind.

Abel drives me to the town hall, where he had put together a library. But I'm too tired to read the titles clearly. I see some Bal-zac, that's enough for me. We walk around his property. I admire the monumental hindquarters of three crossbred Boulonnais horses. The stable contains a dozen or so heifers and a bull. On the opposite

* Émile Guillaumin (1873–1951) was a farmer and writer.

side of the courtyard are more than a hundred white rabbits, like eggs that quiver.

A little after dinner, Abel brings a bottle of Savigny up from the cellar, an excuse for us to talk about Beaujolais and Mâconnais, from where my wife was born and which is for me an adopted home. Abel tells us that in his grandfather's time there were only winegrowers in this region, the Gâtinais. Their wine was bad and they didn't make a good living. Phylloxera came. It looked like disaster, total ruin. The region was saved by phylloxera. Winegrowers stopped growing vines and turned to intensive farming. Now, whoever lives off the land within fifteen kilometers of Montargis lives respectably.

We ate with Abel, Madame Delaveau and their three children. Our adventures, which after all were hardly tragic, amused the whole family. We chatted late after dinner. It was almost midnight when, out of politeness, we got up. Because we were not in a hurry. Nothing was forcing us to leave early the next day. We were a hundred kilometers from Paris. So there were much more than a hundred kilometers between the fighting and us.

Stretched out between the sheets, I feel the mattress with every part of my body and sink voluptuously into a deep sleep.

I'm woken abruptly by a rapping on the door. I recognize Abel's voice. I get up and open the door. Abel is holding a lantern from the stable. The entire room flickers in that flickering glow. "The mayor," Abel says, "received the order to evacuate the village. The men aged sixteen to forty-five. The women can stay."

It's two hours after midnight. It's dark. We deliberate confusedly. Perhaps the wise thing would be to stay, or to leave the women to guard the farm. But it seems impossible for the men to abandon the women. We know nothing about the Germans' conduct except what they did, or what the newspapers attributed to them, in Poland. And from the courtyard we can see the glow of fires in the vicinity of Mignières. These are no doubt villages burning.

We prepare to leave. Madame Delaveau puts the mattresses on the floor and takes some sheets from an armoire. She has tears in her eyes. Her youngest daughter, little Jacqueline, a twelve-year-old, sobs, not wanting to leave without her prettiest dress.

"What should we bring?" Madame Delaveau asks my wife, as if my wife possessed the great secret of evacuations.

The light from the fires is growing. Later we would learn that French troops had set fire to the supply depot in Mignières. Abel harnesses his three Boulonnais to the hay wagons. Then he goes to the stable and untethers the livestock.

II

FROM CHAPELON TO THE LOIRE. BATTLE SCENES

Not a glimmer of dawn on the road from Chapelon to Ladon. A stopped van looks like a faint gray tapestry to me. Its headlights brighten then disappear. I turn mine on full. Some peasants or soldiers in a field nearby shout insults at me. I shut off my headlamps. I turn them on again. Four times, five, maybe more, thanks to which I was able to drive four kilometers in less than an hour.

Day breaks. We find the caravan again. We reinsert ourselves. By evening, we'll have gone about a dozen kilometers.

The stops for bottlenecks are an hour, two hours, I can't recall. We are stuck in front of an abandoned house surrounded by a garden. Through the fence we can see some red-currant bushes. My wife picks a few currants, bringing them back in the palm of her hand. She took great care not to break the branches. But she has just left the garden when a strapping young man in a tunic enters and returns with a trophy of branches. He is at war, one with winners and losers. Our respect for the branches of currant bushes is already anachronistic.

Some military trucks overtake us in a second file. It is a regular convoy, orderly. But their column gets stuck as well.

People from the caravan, those not asleep in their cars, wander the roadsides. An officer pacing back and forth beside a truck asks if we are hungry, if the children are hungry. He has hardtack distributed. His face is grave and sad.

An artilleryman offers me a glass of white wine. I drink it in a single draft. A motorcycle trooper keeps his balance by holding onto the door of a car and demonstrates for a comrade the rules of balancing on a motorbike, showing him which muscle groups are involved. He speaks volubly, extremely nervously. I remember that when the convoy moved off, he blurted out to me, "We're going to do in a few." He believed in a battlefront at the Loire.

"Don't leave any . . . ," I say to him.

I'm not particularly proud of this reply. It expresses my feelings at that moment. I'd willingly have sacrificed several thousand Germans in the abstract for the Loire front not to collapse. Besides, I had said the same thing when the press and French radio announced the capture of Narvik and described thousands of enemy corpses floating in the sea.

The caravan, its peasant carts and its autos, is still stopped. Minutes, hours pass. I can't even say they seem long. These minutes and hours are outside normal time.

From a small, tarpaulin-roofed truck—on the back of which a fifteen-year-old girl is perched bizarrely, like the figurehead on a ship's stern—a shrewish-looking woman emerges. She is chanting: "We've been sold out, we've been betrayed . . ." This common accusation, which I afterward heard often on the road, seemed sufficient in itself. I never got a response to the question: "By whom?" But there is a popular faculty for divination that overwhelms the fumblings of judgment.

The shrew decided to act as the traffic police. Indeed civilian vehicles were jumping the queue, flouting order as well as courtesy. She screams, "You shit . . . bastards . . ." She stands in the middle of the road, arms crossed, and forces a car to stop. The car is driven by a young blond woman with painted eyebrows who is not exactly finding the right words.

"I'm the wife of a gunnery officer . . ."

Describing herself this way elicits jeers, a collective outcry. "Who gives a damn! . . ."

The cars are two abreast, sometimes three. A soldier detailed from who-knows-where tries in vain to unsnarl traffic. This minuscule attempt at policing is the first since Paris. The soldier can do nothing; the harpy insults him. No one objects. The trooper, a good guy, replies that his training was not with a white baton as a traffic cop in Paris, calmly points out that he did not deserve the old woman's insults and that she had been disrespectful to him without cause. Then her husband intervenes, his tone of voice howling in the style of classic tragedy: "With you people she will never be enough . . ." The shrew, now addressing the four winds, demands bread and gasoline. Bread and gasoline; it's like the cry of a mob. I sense the beginnings of a riot on the roadway. It won't occur.

The caravan moves a few meters, stops, moves again. Its links loosen and solidify. With a regimen of twenty restarts an hour for five consecutive days, many starters no longer engage, many batteries are dead. A boy approaches the open hood of a car and observes sadly, "It's all these broke-down cars . . ." Even when there's no mechanical failure, many cars are being pushed by hand simply to save gasoline.

Several cars overtake the caravan at great speed. They are filled with officers. Respectful of the military's priority, the caravan docilely pulls over to the right. At first we would stand at attention for a moment, we would salute these officers who are going ahead to prepare our defense. Except we are a little surprised to see so many women in the military vehicles. But they no doubt belong to the Red Cross. One of the vehicles from the caravan veers a little to the left. An officer leans out, yelling and pointing a revolver at the tires. Stuck to the road like a snail to its rock, the caravan doesn't react.

That's when for the first time I see isolated infantrymen, unoarmed, heads down, dragging their shoes, sometimes their sandals, along the grass on the roadsides. Avoiding a bicyclist, skirting a stopped auto without seeming to see them. Walking like blind men, like disheveled shadows. Strangers to the peasants in their carts, to the city people in their cars, to military units, they are alone, like beggars who have renounced begging. This is the beginning of the rout. We don't realize it. We take them for stragglers; we believe that their regiments are far ahead.

We had left Abel Delaveau's farm before dawn. It's six in the evening. We've gone about a dozen kilometers. At each restart, my wife has to push the car. This distresses me; I'd say it humiliates me—at first.

I am prisoner of a route I didn't choose. I have become a refugee and have no refuge. I'm sleepy. Why keep going? Tomorrow, the traffic will no doubt be better. The horse carts from the Beauce and the Gâtinais, and the cars from Paris, will all have passed. There can't possibly be a single car left in Paris. It's hard to imagine that Paris could have contained so many.

I give up moving with the caravan in fits and starts. I lie down on the grass beside the road. But I don't find the hoped-for rest. The river of carts and automobiles is hypnotic. It streams along beside us, yet absorbs and overwhelms us. There is a beautiful meadow where some cars have already parked. I add ours. We decided to spend the night there.

My wife goes to a farm two hundred meters away to buy a chicken. But the farmwoman's cart is harnessed and she has already taken up the reins. The cows have been let loose, left to themselves, and don't know where to go. The farmwoman shouts to my wife, "Take all the chickens you want."

Two young people who left Paris yesterday evening by motorcycle abandon their machine for lack of gasoline. The news they give is reassuring. "We left in no hurry by the Porte d'Italie. We didn't see any Germans. Maybe there were some at the Porte Maillot, but there were none at the Porte d'Italie . . ."

One of the young people kills the chicken. But he is inexperienced; he did not drain its blood. And we eat the blackish meat, which has a vaguely gamy taste.

I go into a neighboring field to fetch some straw. We arrange it in our meadow to fashion a comfortable bed. It's a beautiful night, moonlit, but not silent. The passing of military vehicles is ceaseless. The rumbling is continuous, like the sound of a waterfall. The night consists of only the moon and the trucks. The following day, Sunday, June 16th, we depart again. To restart after stopping on an incline, I've been getting a push by the car behind me. But the driver warns me that he will no longer be able to help me this way because doing so increases fuel consumption and he is nearly out of gas.

Some policemen and firemen are walking single file on the left-hand side of the road. This is an indication only of the precautionary evacuation of Paris. But the military stragglers are more numerous. Limping, slouched, they are recognizable only by their forage caps as having been soldiers.

For lunch, to eat the rest of the chicken, we stop on a very wide part of the roadside quite near a beautiful farmhouse fronted by two long lawns and surrounded by woods.

We share our meal with a policeman. He had been sitting on the grass. He was coming by bicycle from I don't know where, going I don't know where. We exchange a few words about the current mess. He concludes: "When you see things like this, you ask yourself whether . . ."

And he says no more about it. But the worst of circumstances cannot stifle the genius of those who know how to use people and events in the right combinations. A driver, one of thousands in this bloated caravan, approaches the policeman and says to him, "This can't continue . . . It's a disgrace . . . There is no police presence . . . If you like, I'll load your bicycle onto my car; get on the running board and you can unsnarl the column of traffic."

The policeman accepts and the car drives off alongside the line, passing by like a command car and disregarding the caravan.

A group on the grass, beside a small van, is lunching on canned food. The tone, the accent reek of Paris, or rather the Paris suburbs. A woman in her fifties is very agitated and no longer knows how to speak without shouting. Her words contain all the contradictions of the suburbs and of history itself: "The Germans are people like us. I can never be made to say that the war isn't crap . . . Neither we nor the English are little saints . . . remember how the English treated the Boers . . . That doesn't stop me from having wept when I learned that the Germans were in Paris . . ."

On the road, the traffic jam hasn't eased. Two-wheeled carts, cars lined up for three hundred kilometers with no one directing traffic. But yes . . . there is a police presence, a sergeant. I've never seen brutish like this braying, gangly brute. I don't know whether he's drunk with fright or power. He shouts "To the right" at drivers whose cars are in the roadside ditch. He flings himself into a momentarily empty car, starts the engine, tries to put it into first gear and cannot because he is pushing the accelerator to the floor. By making the gears screech, he imagined he would unsnarl traffic on the road. He abandons the car and attempts to reestablish order generally with another local expedient. A peasant cart driven by a young girl is not completely on the right-hand side of the road. He doesn't give the girl time to turn her horse. He lunges at the animal's head, seizes the rein and pulls on the bit brutally, stunning the horse, frightening the girl and managing to move the cart only a few centimeters to the right.

Then he disappears. This kind of man is no fan of danger. Indeed some airplanes are passing overhead; they drop bombs and fire their machine guns. People lie down in the roadside ditches, hide in the woods or cling to trees in the farmyard. Some children grab their mothers' skirts; the women circle the trees and hide their faces in their arms, like a boy avoiding a slap.

I make out the corduroy pants of a wagoner hiding beneath his wagon. I study their color and the ribbing. My longstanding desire for corduroy pants to wear in the country has reached its climax.

The airplanes have disappeared. We learn that the farmhouse cellar contains two barrels of cider and a cask of eau de vie. So a veritable resupply operation is organized. Those carrying empty bottles cross paths on the lawn with those carrying full bottles. It looks like a labor requisition.

A magnificent procession enters the courtyard: wagons pulled by trains of horses, carts hitched to four or six oxen. But these carts and wagons were not loaded with a miscellaneous freight of mattresses, hay and bicycles like the carts in the caravan. They parade in as if for an agricultural fair, they parade in like the Merovingian chariots of feudal kings in old history textbooks. This impressive procession belongs to the M. family, which owns, it's said, thousands of hectares in the Beauce. It is led by two booted horsemen on sport horses. I didn't know whether they were the owners or the managers of the abandoned estate.

Some drivers, immobilized by lack of gasoline, are begging them for a tow. Nothing could have been easier. Their wagons are very lightly loaded and some are pulled by six oxen, as I mentioned. But they refuse with a disingenuous reluctance, they refuse without saying no, they refuse politely but without warmth. They had a calf slaughtered for them and their drivers, but they weren't concerned about children who for three days have been fed nothing but a little curdled milk.

Fatigue and despondency are keeping us in this somber courtyard. Evening is coming. We have traveled four kilometers since morning. We should go on nonetheless, go somewhere. It appears that the caravan is being directed toward Gien. From Gien, heading east, we could no doubt get to Auxerre, Avallon. But I'm nearly out of gasoline. There's only one solution left: being towed by a truck or horse cart. We would travel as quickly and more surely than if the motor were running. But it's not easy. Many cars are already going in pairs. The military trucks are no longer towing civilian vehicles, as they had the first few days. The peasants' carts are fully loaded with people and things, and their horses couldn't pull anything more. And the cart drivers are reluctant to stop to hitch up: they don't want to lose their place in the crowd.

A dazed, sleepy old man perched high on the seat of an uncovered flatbed cart that is barely loaded agrees to stop. We offer him 500 francs to tow us as far as Gien. He accepts. He brings his rig into the courtyard. To tie up the car, I solicit the help of a peasant. He's Polish. Where is he coming from? He leaves the bridle of his horse with his wife and very skillfully knots the old rope I hand him. He refuses any tip forcefully and with real dignity.

There's nothing left but to set off. We water the horse. We give him some fodder. We watch the horse's meal respectfully, like watching the meal of a lord. The horse is not very docile. "Understand," his master tells me, "it's not that he's mean, but he is crazy. And I don't know how to drive horses . . . This horse belongs to my son, who is a scrap-iron dealer . . . And my son told me to take the horse to Carcassone."

I assume that once he is on the road, the horse will follow the line. But before the roadway there's a ditch on the right that worries me and does not seem to worry the old man on his seat. Nevertheless, the horse, the cart and the car get under way. This horse is crazy, but he's courageous. Here we are en route, in line. We travel some hundred meters in the dark. I've rarely felt such contentment at the wheel of a car. But the caravan stops. Restarting, the rope breaks. I call out in the dark for the old man to stop his horse. We reattach the rope; it breaks again. But this time the old man, who is asleep on his seat, doesn't hear me. I never saw him again.

I can hardly expect to continue on my own. At this speed the radiator is sure to boil over. I leave the car to my wife and Andrée F.* I stretch out in the field; the caravan passes by like a nightmare. I fall asleep.

I'm woken. Some soldiers, sent from Lorris no doubt by some vague police authority, want to push my car to the shoulder. I sit at the wheel. They push so hard that had I not violently hit the brakes, I'd have gone into the ditch.

The car is stopped halfway on the grass and halfway on the edge of the shoulder. Because of the shoulder and the wheels buried in the grass, my wife and Andrée F. won't be able to move the car. Plus it's nighttime, the cars in the caravan are blind, which is to say it's impossible to catch the attention of a driver, to kindle the slightest innate sympathy, the slightest wish to help.

The caravan to our left stops. I plead with the driver of a cart who is holding his horse by the bridle to tow me at least up onto the roadway. He hesitates, he parleys with his wife, who is driving the following cart. But in the meantime he entrusts me with his horse. I take the bridle. But this enormous beast will not stop lifting its muzzle toward the sky. "He's not mean; he's stupid," the peasant told me. I'm unlucky: the other horse was crazy; this one is stupid. Even though I'm very scared of the horse, I remain bravely at my post, I stay for a long time. It's one way to woo the farmer, who'll perhaps agree to help me. He returns. I understand clearly that he would like nothing more than to help me. But his wife does not want to. Standing in her cart, she invokes the Loire, the Loire that they must reach in order to at last be safe from all harm.

* The Werths' son's nanny.

For the Loire is now the desired goal, fluvial and strategic, that the collective soul of the caravan has set for itself. "The moment we cross the Loire, we'll calm down . . . ," a peasant woman said. It seems all the peasant women in France had taken courses at the War College.

Dawn is breaking. We left Paris seven days ago. Two young men, mechanics, free me from my grassy slope. A wagoner driving a tumbrel harnessed to two horses agrees to tow me. Since Montereau the landscape has seemed featureless to us, sparse, faded, miserable. Maybe it was the effect of our fatigue, of our interrupted sleep.

Our wagoner stops his horses. He has seen a dead horse in a meadow. Calmly, taking his time, as if he were at a blacksmith's, he removes its horseshoes. This wagoner may not know war, but he knows the road and he knows horses. He's in no rush. Neither are we. We are sleepy.

But the caravan, until then patient, is now aggressive, shaking with fear, mistrust and hatred. The motorists complain that the horse-cart drivers are slowing progress; the horse-cart drivers criticize the motorists for thinking they have the right to do anything, "and yet it is we who provide you with food . . ."

The caravan is inhabited by two moral entities called the Loire and the fifth column. The Loire is the guardian angel that awaits some thirty kilometers away. The fifth column is the free-floating entity, a detestable divinity that incarnates and disincarnates, appearing and disappearing ten times in five minutes. The fifth column is everything (beings and objects), everything that stands between the refugees and the Loire. The fifth column is the frenzy of intolerance in this once-sedentary population suddenly become nomads.

The caravan has stopped among meadows that rise upward toward a horizon of thin woods, that rise on dreary slopes like the oblique planes of some elementary geometry. Some automobiles, in order to overtake, are crossing the fields. Everything is bottlenecked. A refugee, sweating, with a lost look in his eyes, runs alongside the caravan, his briefcase in hand, shouting to us as he passes, "It's too much, they called me a spy."

Behind us a sort of emaciated, disheveled sibyl prophesizes in obscure terms. My wife approaches to put some questions to her.

She replies, "I beg you to go your own way . . . I have nothing to say to you and you well know it. Take your precautions as I have my safeguards. I know what is and what it's all about . . . You know better than I where you come from and what your obligations are. I ask you to make way."

Otherwise, these people aren't crazy enough to invoke tutelary deities and beasts of the apocalypse. Everything since Paris is inexplicable by the laws of reason. We are made to take roundabout routes, to trace gyrating kilometers around towns and forests in order to leave the highways to military convoys. Nonetheless, we are constantly mixed together with military convoys . . . We even wonder why the enemy aircraft bomb and strafe so moderately. Perhaps because bombing, in halting a section of the caravan, would take the place of the absent traffic police, reducing the congestion, disorder and chaos. This free-for-all is so total, so enduring, so absolute that it cannot be entirely attributable to our headquarters no matter how unstrung it might be, nor to the planning of enemy spies, however numerous or organized they might be.

I'm sleepy. Hundreds of thousands of evacuees, of refugees, driven out by the authorities or departing voluntarily, hundreds of thousands of impromptu nomads are sleepy like me. I proceed, towed by the tumbrel's two monumental horses. I have never seen such a landscape, a landscape of ashes. It is vast, spare and pathetically macabre. I hesitate to use the word *macabre*, which forcefully implies something horrible, something emphatic of death. Maybe it's the tree limbs, not pallid and limp but rather etched in spindly lines. It's nothing but a field, the dreariest of all the fields in the world. Two immobile horses gaze out at the road, meditating rather, taking in the endless line of traffic that no longer surprises but still hypnotizes them. One of the two, upright on its four hooves, its harness tied to a tree, is dead.

The tumbrel moves on, pulling us along for three or four kilometers. (I can say that today, having consulted a map.) And we are three or four kilometers from Ouzouer-sur-Loire. But I no longer reckon distance in kilometers nor time in hours. I perceive only alternations between immobility and movement, between day and night.

At a bend in the road surrounded by brush fifty meters from an isolated house, we stop again. My wife and Andrée F. get out of the car to relax and, without much hope, to ask the inhabitants of the house whether any bread or milk might be found. I stay behind alone, resting against the steering wheel, enjoying the silence. Evening is falling; the light is sad and soft. I don't know whether I'm drowsy or meditating. Suddenly there's a crackle of machine-gun fire. I don't know exactly where it's coming from. It is nearby and raking the ground. Every note of this symphony of clacks is distinct despite the speed of its cadence; each has its full resonance. It was as if the entire space had contracted to a single point and exploded into clatter. I see nothing but the back of the tumbrel and the empty roadway. I don't have time to contemplate for long. Mortar rounds coming from I don't know where are exploding I don't know where. The lead carthorse I'm attached to rears; the second does the same out of politeness. And with that, they bolt. Should I confess that in an instant I forgot about my wife and Andrée F.? My shock at the first bursts of machine-gun fire was no doubt fear. But I'm no longer afraid. I'm being pulled by a force over which I have no control, to which I am, what can I say? directly tied, attached by a rope. It was so unexpected and quick that I hadn't time to feel afraid. It was irresistible, like a fall from the top of the towers of Notre-Dame must be. And, it must be said, the exodus had been dull, like trench warfare was, dull and monotonous. In the trenches in 1914, boredom predominated over death. I'm aware of the simplistic lyricism of this, which resembles a battle painting and those games children invent, when they tie improvised wagons and chariots together. All the more so as the first horse, its front hooves seeming so light suspended in the air, rears with an enthusiasm inspired by historic paintings and equestrian sculptures. He's not rearing anymore; he's galloping. We're flying. It has been a long time since I moved so fast. I feel as if I'm part of some cavalry charge in the battle of Reichshoffen.

My natural caution kept me from relishing the frenzy for long. I steered the car into the last vehicle of a stopped column. My front fenders locked with its back fenders. Dead stop. The rope had broken.

Ahead of me the wagon was moving at great speed. It plunged into the roadside ditch and I saw the lead horse lying on its side at the edge of the roadway.

I get out of the car, whose front end is pinned. Behind the car, a dead horse. It is one of an artillery van's horses that, without my hearing or feeling it, had collapsed, smashing and partly ripping away a fender. When, how had it fallen? I don't know. What projectile had hit it? I have no idea. Its head lies on the road, jutting toward the middle, where a trickle of blood is spreading. The car cannot be accessed by someone coming from the farmhouse without stepping over the horse's head.

My wife and Andrée F. had barely left the car when German soldiers lined the roadway and, firing at the machine gunner, closed the road to Lorris to the French artillerymen and the civilians mixed in with them. The two women take cover in a field where two Germans are extending the line of riflemen. One of the two stops firing and signals the women to take shelter in a little wood at the left of the field. And he says to the other in French, yes, in French, and quite good French: "Don't shoot . . . there are too many women and children . . ."

But the little wood is far. The two women run as far as a ditch where some people, women and children, are already crouching. Two other women, as if reciting litanies in a chapel, endlessly repeat aloud, "Saint Christopher . . . pray for us." An artilleryman hides himself among the crouching and kneeling civilians. But the ditch isn't very deep. Their backs are exposed. My wife and Andrée F. take cover beneath a small van. But their legs are exposed, and they feel stones, as if fired from a slingshot, ricocheting at their feet. My wife feels a burning in her calf. It's no more than a small, bleeding wound, where a sliver of metal has lodged. But two artillery horses are down, and their bodies, screening the bottom of the little van, are protecting my wife and Andrée F. from gunfire.

That was in the space of a few minutes. My wife is worried about me. She is sure that, dragged by the horses, I have been crushed beneath the car. Andrée F. quickly reassures her.

My wife emerges, crawling. Night has fallen. In the darkness some of the wounded are collected; they are helped into automobiles and carts, which make U-turns and speed off in the direction of Lorris.

The Germans are still shooting, but they don't seem to be aiming at the space between the road and the farm. A French artilleryman, wounded in the leg, is limping, leaning on my wife's shoulder, toward the farmhouse.

I don't know how we found each other again, near the car. We have just sat down when some Germans appear, Indian file, in helmets and armed with machine guns. They are coming not from the direction of Lorris, which is to say from Paris, but from the direction of Ouzouer, which is to say from the Loire. Not only had they caught up with us, but they had also passed us and were doubling back. They had simply overtaken us by traveling through the woods.

They are walking five meters apart. They pass near the car. Never during the war of 1914 had I seen Germans from this close except as prisoners. None are the fleshy German type, grossly made. They look at us while passing. We look at them, too. Later, my wife said to me, "I couldn't believe they were Germans; they looked like Japanese fighters to me . . ." This poetic logic was accurate. Their features are contorted, taut. Their wincing makes them look Asian below the helmet. This is understandable. They are afraid, and they push on. This mixture of worry and resolve is, strictly speaking, military courage. They push on, and nothing impedes them. They are no doubt as astonished about it as I am. They are no doubt expecting some trap. They number no more than about thirty. The column halts. One of the soldiers stops in front of the car door. His face becomes visible, framed by the window. This face-to-face, this proximity, is uncomfortable. And this discomfort goes beyond worry or fear. I have the urge to kill this man, or to talk to him about the weather or his health. My wife murmured a few words I don't recall, to ward off silence, or death. Rather stupidly I tell her, "This man has no desire to kill us." For a few seconds the three of us form a group at the margins of the war. Perhaps even some fleeting sympathy passed between him and us like a ripple on water. And it seemed to me that the shadow of a smile glided across his clenched features.

Guarded by two German soldiers, a number of civilians are assembled on the roadside. Their hands are in the air. On a signal by the Germans, their arms are lowered. But a young man with a mournful face obstinately raises his arms higher with a distorted gymnastic motion, his open palms facing the sky. No doubt he's thinking that an excess of caution can't hurt, and no doubt he's afraid lest the Germans imagine he has decided to die fighting. It's sad and funny. At last, one of the soldiers, his hand exaggeratedly patting the air, reassures him: "Enough . . . enough."

A few women are gathered between the front of the farmhouse and an impassable line of two helmeted Germans. Perhaps the women can no longer bear their mute, paralyzing fear, their anxiety over a danger no longer associated with noise. As for what comes next, I can't pretend to explain, only recount. At this moment, the women raise their arms. I don't know whether they conferred or whether the cry rises spontaneously from their throats. At any rate, they are whimpering more than shouting: "Search us! Search us!"

Do they mean to say that they are not hiding any guns under their skirts; are they offering the conqueror the money or jewelry they're carrying to appease him? Is it a simple plea, a cry to ward off evil?

One of the Germans regards them coldly and says in French, "You are female prisoners . . . you will be subject to the same fate as German women . . ."

This "you will be subject to the same fate" has something solemn, ridiculous, like a grammar exercise. And its meaning seems obscure to me. Are these peasant women being threatened with harsh Germanic discipline or are they being reassured, persuaded that German women are not so unhappy after all?

Fifty meters on, toward Ouzouer, some French artillerymen are gathered close together forming a human bundle, an opaque and shapeless mass.

The women huddled against the farmhouse wall yell to them, "Surrender! Surrender! There are children." An unnecessary request. All at once, as much by clear decision as from fear, they raise their hands.

I don't value military courage much, but I felt shame. This was the only time, in my whole life I believe, that I felt a personal military passion, a desire to fight.

I am recounting what I saw and what I felt. I'm not attempting a historical reconstruction or an after-the-fact narrative, coherent and critical, of military operations. At these moments I knew nothing about the whole in which this incident has its place. Watching from the farmhouse wall, believing myself to be a prisoner, I couldn't even tell whether those artillerymen who had so little fight in them gathered there like a troop of lost dogs, whether any officer were with them, whether they even form a military unit. I don't know whether the nomadic infantrymen on the roadsides and the fragmented artillery convoys hadn't received an order or an example that, in plain language, could only be translated as, "Bolt whenever you want, whenever you can, and block up the Loiret . . ."

The Germans and the artillerymen prisoners have hardly left when a few horse-drawn French artillery caissons arrive. A hidden unit of Germans fires on the convoy. The towrope of a gun carriage at the end of the convoy comes undone, the caisson teeters then falls into the roadside ditch. An artilleryman runs to the horses' heads, others put their shoulders to the wheels. An officer takes the place of the man holding the bridle, lifts the head of one of the horses and gives it some support using the bit. All this under fire.

But the women near the farmhouse wall, as they did earlier, shout at the officer and his men, "Surrender! Surrender!"

"We have nothing to do with civilians . . . ," the officer, a young lieutenant, responds.

The women are shouting, but their shouting is only a lament. Their fear, a tantrum of fear, makes them shout and prompts this extraordinary ellipsis: "Cowards . . . cowards . . . surrender."

The men are leaning into the wheels, bracing themselves against the ground; the horse rears one last time convulsively, comes down again and, exhausted or hit by a bullet, collapses on its side. Only then do the artillerymen abandon the effort; that's how, that night, honor was preserved.

It's now pitch-dark. The officer and the artillerymen approach the farm. I was told that an old peasant embraced them.

The officer asks us where the Germans came from and in which direction they left. They're nowhere to be seen. They hid in the woods and advanced toward Ouzouer.

Despite the darkness, I make out the handsome features of a firm, kind face. I was concentrating only on giving him information, but I too wanted to embrace that young man, who may have already known that all was lost but who wanted to lose nobly.

I have recounted these events piecemeal, disconnected from each other. A little more geography perhaps might have made it clearer, but more like a report, slowing down and further distorting the narrative. It would have been clearer still if I took into account what we discovered later: that is to say, that the Germans knew the terrain perfectly, as well as the size, route and distribution of our convoys. Moreover, a raw transcription of events is impossible. Event, emotion and opinion comingle. However faithful a report might be, it gives a beginning and end to what has neither, and transforms it into theater. It explains and rationalizes an event that is accompanied by neither commentary nor explanation and has no concern for rational justifications.

When the shooting stopped, when the evening silence came, I felt a sort of absurd satisfaction. During the 1914 war, during months in the trenches, I saw nothing that as much resembled war as it appears in legends and images.

Today I have difficulty imagining what we understood of the military situation, the distance we assumed was between the bulk of enemy troops and us. I think we very much believed in a vanguard of motorcyclists or even parachutists, dispatched like cavalry scouts in the old days. The way at the beginning of the 1914 war we had seen innocuous patrols of uhlans. We had no idea whatsoever of the total breakdown of French forces. We assumed they were awaiting the enemy on the far bank of the Loire. And all the convoys that had overtaken us could only have one mission: to reinforce resistance at the Loire.

Witnesses to the unbelievable chaos, we were not assessing its effects. This exodus, this mélange of soldiers and civilians, city people and peasants, suddenly appeared before us like the acute stage of an illness, like a storm. An absurd hope was born from a no less absurd, almost instinctive logic, from a bizarre denial of the evidence. It was impossible that nothing had been planned for the end point of this rout. This rout was itself proof that the high command had taken other measures. Its negligence here was proof of its vigilance elsewhere. And who knows whether the Germans, who were gaining on us, who were at our heels, had not been pulled into a trap? Perhaps they would be taken prisoner? We were convinced that we could be captured, but not France.

We enter the farmhouse. It is filled with an unrelated group of people: apparently peasants and city people traveling on foot, caught in the violence. The farm is abandoned; its inhabitants have left. Some old people are seated on a bench behind a table. On a bed in the back a wounded soldier is laid out; he had been hit in the arm and near the heart. He's bleeding. He's not responding to questions. It's unclear whether he is about to die. An old woman, an octogenarian at least, sitting on a chair in a corner, thinks only of getting up to go for a little walk along the road. Her family watches over her with indulgence and firmness. She rises halfway and points out to me the wounded man on the bed, which is obscured by people wandering around the room: "I would like to know how that young man is doing . . ." I find a spot on the bench, lean my elbows on the table and sleep.

It's impossible to think of leaving in the pitch dark. It's impossible to sleep in this crowd. We decide to rest in the hayloft, which can be reached by a ladder. The hayloft is cement and contains neither hay nor straw. No matter. To lie down is a luxury. But at the other end of the loft an old woman, in a voice both furious and monotonous, is shouting insults and reproaches at her daughter-in-law and son, endlessly, without pause.

Between night and dawn we decide to set off, and we leave the hayloft.

The car is trapped between the dead artillery-wagon horse and the rear end of another automobile, which is enmeshed with another, which is similarly wedged in, and so on for two hundred meters. Even if I succeed in extricating it from this inextricable line, we won't go far, the gas tank is nearly empty. A bicyclist is shivering in his shirtsleeves and asks whether we couldn't give him a jacket or covering. We have only a white woolen blanket. He puts it over his shoulders and leaves on foot, bent over his machine, looking like a ghost.

We deliberate in this sooty dawn, next to the dead horse, which is now scarcely more to us than an embankment or a mile marker. We quickly decide to continue on foot. That means opening all the suitcases and gathering a little clothing in the smallest. As a household move, it's complicated. Like all men, I'm a coward when faced with moving house. I lose interest. I have only one concern, which is to bring *Terre des hommes*. Not because it is a luxury edition—I have little regard for beautiful editions—but because Saint-Exupéry gave it to me, because the beautiful paper, the uncut pages, aren't sumptuousness and vanity but friendship. Because Saint-Exupéry wrote in it, in his ethereal handwriting, a few words with which my friendship refreshes itself as if at a spring, a few words I would be proud of, were friendship not above pride.

I owe *Terre des hommes* as much worry as joy. When I had to ask for shelter, I entrusted my copy to the host, who hid it on the highest shelf of an armoire under a pile of sheets. Later, having thought about it, and believing I'd be able to get back on the road, I thought it would be safer if I took it with me. Unable to leave, I entrusted it to my host again; then I took it back. Saint-Ex, how you complicated our exodus!

If we have to abandon the car, we'll abandon it farther on. In either case, it will be ransacked. Might as well use every last drop of gasoline. I can't recall how we freed it. But a man got up on the running board and helped us. His wife and their five children disappeared the evening before, during the battle. He started out with two families who were friends; the drivers of both cars had disappeared.

Yesterday's fight cleared the road. We're moving freely. All I remember is a peasant screaming and rolling on the ground; a man was trying to restrain him. We arrive at Ouzouer. But in the middle of the town the road is riddled with holes from mortars and is impassable. We turn onto a byroad that also leads to Gien, the Gien bridge and the Loire, which is stopping the enemy armies.

I've said little or nothing about the cars abandoned by the road-side, in the roadside ditch, upright or on their sides. So I have not given an accurate image of a landscape strewn with automobiles, like a wasteland strewn with tin cans. I've also said nothing about those who abandoned them. But from a distance I won't affect a pity that I no longer felt at the time and that had turned into cold observation. Men, women and children had become pedestrians. It was nothing more than a change in classification, as irrelevant as troop movements. I had acquired the indifference of a soldier or emigrant.

Past Ouzouer, carts and automobiles are returning toward Ouzouer and Lorris, that is, heading away from the Loire. People are shouting to us that the Loire can no longer be crossed and that the Gien bridge had blown up.

My wife decides to cross the Loire at all costs, no matter how, by swimming if need be. I admire her for still planning and for aspiring to influence fate. Everything seems so absolutely incoherent to me that it no longer seems possible to bring any rational calculus or human volition to bear.

The countryside is bare and seems uninhabited. We see only deserters, nomads. This area is just a desert track.

An airplane passes overhead and strafes by approximation, none too insistently. People flee into the roadside ditch and the woods.

A whimpering man in his fifties, a doctor from near Paris, abandoned his car for lack of gasoline. He brought neither suitcase nor knapsack nor bundle. There is a consolation in desperation, which is to part with everything, to be reduced to oneself. He's not losing his misery in the misery of others. He takes refuge in his; he takes refuge in his complaints, in his tears. He is alone; he's wandering straight ahead. Even so, he's whining about having left behind I don't recall what book. It's touching and a little comic, for as I remember it was over one of those "deluxe" editions, with cheap illustrations, that were mass-produced after the 1914 war.

I had reassured two peasant women with a young girl coming from who knows where. I had told them, knowing nothing and completely at random, that we had little chance of being hit by bullets from an airplane. We tell each other our misfortunes. They suggest we take shelter with them in a certain abandoned farmhouse well away from the road. The Germans won't think to go there. We'll live there "while waiting." There are beds and, in a field next to the house, hay and potatoes. Chickens are still pecking in the farmyard and a cow, fussing in the meadow, wants only to be looked after.

Many people lived that way, for days and days. It was not an absurd plan. But the Germans neglected neither winding country roads nor isolated houses. The idea of a rustic life away from the flood of refugees tempts me. But we wanted to cross the Loire.

My wife learns from an old peasant that nearby is a mill and a ferryman. Our decision is made. We'll beg the miller to look after the car and we'll cross with three small suitcases, which we will make as light as possible, since afterwards we must travel by foot.

III

LES DOUCIERS.
FIFTH COLUMN

The peasant was an Arab storyteller. On his directions, five hundred meters from the Loire we find a sandy courtyard and a low house. There is indeed an old mill not far away, but nothing had been milled in it for a long time. The ferryman, there since the day before, is a refugee from Paris who had taken a few soldiers across the Loire.

I learn this from a very brunette, slightly reticent woman who makes little faces while speaking. The house belongs to her. Her husband stayed in Courbevoie, where he manages a factory. Their apartment was bombed; the bombs did significant damage to it, in particular shattering windowpanes that cost 4,000 francs each. It's true that a man from Paris, who is an acquaintance of hers, ferried some soldiers across and will perhaps consent to take us across as well. She agrees to lend one of her rowboats provided that the other, which a refugee left on the opposite side of the river, can be brought back, because each of these boats is worth 3,500 francs, "and thirty-five hundred francs is not a sum one throws into the Loire."

I also learn that two soldiers borrowed a ladder to cross the Loire. They got into the water holding onto the uprights. But one of them drowned.

I admired the blossoms of some rosebushes planted in front of the house on the other side of the courtyard. I genuinely admire them but say so also to be attentive, for I'm the guest, the supplicant.

I learn that they grow thanks only to the care of an old gardener, a nice old man, but one who works very slowly and to whom she pays seven francs an hour.

I am, I admit, a little irritated by this numerical evaluation of every object, by this transcribing of the world into prices. It seems too simplistic to me to see only vulgarity and a poor education here. This is irresistible and persistent, like a tic; I think it must be some sort of disease.

Moreover, Madame Soutreux's welcome has a tense, mannered kindness, a kindness without warmth. But after all, by what right could we demand that she give us her heart? She isn't refusing us access to her courtyard. She will introduce us to the mysterious, benevolent ferryman; she agrees that we can leave our car in her yard provided, of course, it won't be for too long (this goes without saying and seems fair). She also agrees to watch over a few things that are precious to us.

Besides, it is she who holds the secret of the Loire; she is the goddess of the Loire. And we wish to cross the Loire at all costs. To cross the Loire, I'm prepared for any concession, any indulgence. That is why I offer to swim across the river to fetch the 3,500-franc rowboat still on the other shore.

We ready our bundles for the crossing and for our new journey on foot.

But an artillery duel begins over our heads. The French mortar shells fall near Ouzouer and the Germans' shells hit the evacuated villages on the other side of the river. A rocket lands in the courtyard.

We no longer think of crossing the Loire.

Madame Soutreux offers hospitality. She gives us permission to stay in her courtyard and sleep in the car.

We are strangers. We appeared suddenly at this house, far from the main road, reachable only by a crude, rutted track. It is an ancient farmhouse consisting of a ground floor, level with the courtyard, and a shed topped by a hayloft. Its transformation into a Sunday pied-à-terre for Parisians is very recent. Only a single room has been furnished, which Madame Soutreux uses as both a dining room and a bedroom. The walls of the other rooms have not yet been papered and the doors not yet painted. In one of the rooms there is a bed frame.

Madame Soutreux does not inhabit this vast, barely furnished house alone. People are moving around the courtyard and inside the house who seem familiar with the place and "fully authorized." The most mediocre observer would grasp immediately that they form a temporary group and that they are strangely dissimilar. Some are nearly unclassifiable. The majority of novelists rely on a base of stable, well-defined mores. Their characters move toward or away from the customary. But in France since 1914, prejudices have weakened as much as their premises. Mores and social relationships have lost all solidity. Weak personalities have become incoherent, and this very incoherence lends them an apparent originality.

For eight days we lived among people some of whom seemed nearly inexplicable to us. At least surprising enough for us to be unable to readily describe them. I'm saying that only a Balzac, if that, could have brought some coherence to this group while leaving them their individuality—and would the times have let him?

Only the Aufresnes are perfectly legible to us, and their feelings are the only ones here that are not as strange to us as those of a Martian or a moon man. Formerly the manager of a department in a department store, Aufresne had set up on his own. Heavyset, he is a common type of Frenchman with average ideas who has kept his parents' values and neither retained nor acquired any others, and who has, since 1920, known no other worry or inspiration than those of an automobile and country inns. He is measured in his speech, firm even. And not without courage. It is he who helps French soldiers cross the Loire, aware of the risk of being denounced or the sudden arrival of the Germans.

His wife had refinement and charm and, as what comes later in the story will show, a heart. They had arrived the day before with their daughter, a very young woman, and granddaughter, a two-year-old.

They had not left Paris bound for Les Douciers, but Aufresne remembered, while in the worst of a traffic jam and a failing piston rod, that he was acquainted with Monsieur Soutreux and knew the location of Les Douciers, having spent a Sunday there. They sleep in the shed.

Madame Lerouchon, wife of a garage owner, has been staying at Les Douciers for quite some time. But she is living with her mother in a trailer parked in the field adjoining the courtyard. She is from Metz and speaks German as fluently as French. Madame Lerouchon resembles a fairground wrestler; she has the bulk and jowly muzzle of one. She doesn't know how to speak without shouting nor how to shout without the accompaniment of a furious pantomime, a pantomime that is not only gesticulation but a simultaneous forward propulsion of her entire body, her head and the simultaneous and separate forward propulsion of her lips. She speaks the way farm dogs bark, for whom barking is not a sign of anger but of excitement, and who wag their tails at the same time as they make themselves heard. I have no reason to say this woman was disagreeable. Worse than that, or something else entirely.

Her niece resembles those "Gretchens" represented in French imagery around 1891: eyes like porcelain and blond plaits.

In the yard, in the house, a busy old man walks about always wearing a soft black hat and an off-white duster. His gaunt face resembles a skull, but a skull shorn of everything macabre, with neither death nor life, a moronic skull. His Midi accent, authentic though it may be, is so exaggerated that it seems put on. Everyone calls him "*le vieux monsieur*," and no one knows him by any other name.

He speaks often of his son, a mechanic who is on the highway charitably repairing cars that break down.

The slow war of the first few months, as I experienced it in Paris, sometimes seemed to me like a war distant in time for the Parisians, a war refrigerated by a history textbook. During the very first days I heard a grocer from Combs-la-Ville, who the next day had to get back to his warehouse, declaring as he taped paper to his windows that he very much hoped to chop Adolf's block off. I'm no longer hearing anything of the kind; I'm seeing only the calm of a self-possessed people. Germans no longer cut off children's hands. The French no longer possess the slice of toast with magic jam that was going to trap the Germans like flies on glue so absolutely effectively that all tactics and strategy were superfluous. The passions of a people aren't easily summed up, but it seemed as if the French had clearly concluded that at this moment in history Germany was the enemy. At Madame Soutreux's I first understood that this could be otherwise.

Head, mouth and lips forward, Madame Lerouchon shouted at the volume of a domestic argument.

"You believe everything you're told about Hitler. But you're told nothing about Chamberlain." Then, in a higher register, her final words screamed like a tenor heaving himself toward the high C, she repeated, "You were told . . . you were told . . . you were told . . . you were told . . . you were told that Hitler was malicious . . . But what do you know about it? . . . What harm do you expect him to do you? . . ."

Madame Lerouchon was seemingly in a frenzy. But it wasn't a towering frenzy. It was a sort of good-girl's frenzy, a fit, a frenzy without malice.

With a certain plebeian power, but with repulsive banality, she presented a savage Chamberlain and a decent Hitler, translating themes from Radio Stuttgart into cartoon images.

Madame Soutreux cannot possibly have grasped our surprise and distaste. It seemed as if she wanted to explain and comment on Madame Lerouchon's words. Hers was a different tone of voice, a sugary little tone. She was speaking with pursed lips. And her words were much less operatic, without apparent passion. She also defended Hitler and Germany, but with the appearance of impartiality and by means of those historical abstractions that are at the disposal of everyone who reads the newspapers.

"Germany was deprived of all its colonies," she said, "it was forced to prepare its revenge. Germany needs to expand in proportion to its population. You must not listen to only one version, you must see both sides . . . You must understand that the Germans are organizers . . ."

After a week of worry and insomnia, we found respite, a refuge, in a French household. The words we were hearing there seemed hallucinatory. But for the moment, I'm not looking for any explanations, I'm scrupulously recounting, in its natural order, reality.

While these two women were speaking, I was remembering that
military tribunals in Paris had sentenced "defeatists" to months or
years in prison, some of whom had expressed nothing but innocent
doubt. I attended one of those hearings. Poor buggers were judged
severely, along vague lines, for having asserted in a bar that train-
loads of wounded were heading toward Paris. I also heard Pastor
Roser condemned to five years in prison for asserting that war was
irreconcilable with the Gospel. But these two women were testifying
to their devotion to Germany in a tone that had nothing confidential
about it, concealing nothing, as if it were the expression of some
orthodox truth.

That is when two German soldiers appeared in the courtyard.
Armed, for sure, but alone, neither fearing nor threatening anyone,
in some way like hikers. They seemed to me more frightening than
those who had machine-gunned us the day before at Ouzouer. At
Ouzouer we were caught up in the risks, the hazards of war. We were
in the violence and noise of war, in the uncertainty that someone
who does not fear death too much can overcome. But these two isolated soldiers were an entire army, covering the entire battleground;
we were all prisoners of these two soldiers. Yesterday's could have
killed us, these could humiliate us.

They only wanted to refill their canteens with water from the well.
But Madame Soutreux wouldn't hear of it. She went down to the cellar and brought them a bottle of wine. She engaged them in cordial
conversation. She spoke German so fluently that I couldn't make out
a single word of what she said.

The two Germans leaned over the Aufresnes' baby, and one of
them took her in his arms. Since then I have always seen German
soldiers act like born nursemaids in front of children, showing the
liveliest tenderness. I'm certainly not claiming that this tenderness
is faked. Even less do I believe that it runs all that deep. And I'm
sure they're mixing in a portion of either unconscious histrionics or
concerted decision. This is how the Germans give proof of their advanced civilization. The kindness of these two toward the baby wasn't
fully exempt from some intent toward propaganda and display. The
soldier who had taken the infant in his arms set it down, saying to

her, "You see . . . your *Boches*,* your barbarians." This, it goes without saying, was directed toward us and not Madame Soutreux, who
stood with them and seemed to gloat over the benevolence of her
helmeted guests.

I'll add that I never saw a German, before taking an infant in his
arms, trouble himself to find out whether this was agreeable or not
to the parents. You'd think the infant belonged to them by right of
conquest.

A half hour later two more soldiers entered the courtyard. Madame Soutreux had not welcomed us with such unreserved, expan-
sive kindness. She became animated; she was in a state of jubilation.
And I wondered whether her jubilation came from speaking with
Germans or speaking German. I came to wonder whether Madame
Soutreux wasn't simply obsessed with foreign languages. That was
when I witnessed one of those spectacles that make you say I can't
believe my eyes. Madame Soutreux came back from the cellar and
she was carrying two glasses and a bottle of champagne. She poured
it into the glasses herself and handed them to the two soldiers. And
she watched them drink with a smiling tenderness.

"*Goot kvality* . . . ," said one of the soldiers to thank her.

That's exactly what happened.

An hour later, another soldier entered the yard. He wasn't as
lucky: The Soutreux woman wasn't there; he got only water.

He was sweating and reeling, not from drunkenness but from
fatigue. Arms outstretched, he held two canteens toward us. I still
don't know what he meant by this gesture. Was he asking where the
well was? Or, as warlord, was he ordering us to bring him water, to
fill them ourselves? Aufresne took the canteens, went to the well,
refilled them and brought them back to the soldier. His face was
tense, flushed, but not one of those that is easily read. Aufresne and
I never exchanged a word about it, then or later. I think he was saying to himself, "I'm obeying the law of the conqueror . . . I'm giving
in to coercion."

I'm saying to myself, "I would sooner get myself killed than go

* Derogatory slang for Germans.

find water for this soldier." I'm sincere and I'm lying. Had the soldier pointed his gun at me, I'd have gone to the well and brought back the canteens. The truth is, at that moment and no other, this soldier and no other would have gone to the well to refill his own canteens without a word had I pointed the way. But everything would have been different had the soldier been a drunk thug or had headquarters decided to instill terror.

A childish discussion . . . you might say. A trivial event, but the discussion is essential. Dignity isn't measured arithmetically. The smaller the event, the better one grasps the nuances of freedom and dignity. I sensed at that moment that I belonged to a people who were recognizing nuances. I remembered that while I was doing my military service an adjutant called to me in the courtyard and ordered me to go to his room and polish his shoes. I refused. Having exhausted threats of the rigors of the Military Code, he gave in to astonishment and a sort of curiosity that I must call psychological. I explained to him that the act of shining shoes seemed in no way beneath me, that I willingly polished my barracks mate's shoes if he was late for inspection or too drunk to do this task himself, but I would not be ordered to shine shoes. I was not shot or punished.

At nightfall, the bombardment begins again. I forgot to say that the house wasn't built on a cellar; what I called a cellar earlier was only a kind of storage space at ground level. We took shelter there, the Aufresnes and us, Madame Soutreux and the Lerouchon woman. That's when we saw two soldiers appear suddenly out of the darkness. I don't know whether they were two from that afternoon—the ones who got wine or the ones who got champagne—or two new ones, whether their coming is their own idea or if some authority sent them. I don't know and I'll never know. The soldiers explain in German to Soutreux and Lerouchon that the house is endangered by the shellfire, that it is reckless to stay here, and they signal all of us to follow them.

So here we are under the Germans' protection. I very much want to stay behind. But I think I ought to choose the least risk for my wife. And anyway, Lerouchon, the good girl, is shouting at me, "So come . . . it has nothing to do with politics . . ." I don't know whether my feelings are political or not. But I give in to the absurdity of a memorable statement and reply to the Lerouchon woman that at this moment she cannot imagine how much I prefer French soldiers to German soldiers. I believe I even had the weakness to add that it wasn't a matter of politics or patriotism, but of dignity . . . My wife, with a great deal of common sense, shuts me up.

We follow the Germans. We cross some fields. It's dark. We haven't eaten anything since morning. One of the fields is cut by a ditch at least two meters deep. The soldiers climb in, sinking knee-high into water. One of them takes the baby in his arms. They help the women get across.

We arrive at a farmhouse where the Germans are billeting. We sit down on the steps of a kind of porch. Heavy shadows are passing through the courtyard. A few of these shadows approach us, join our group. There's some rapid conversation between the shadows, Soutreux and Lerouchon.

Lerouchon makes sure to translate the essence of the conversation for us. The Germans are giving her information about the war. She shouts to us, in a tone of triumph, "They've bombed Dreux; they've bombed Juvisy . . ." She shouts this to us as if she were announcing both a victory for her own country and a personal triumph. Then we can only hear a few sounds, at once raucous and muffled, a torrent of accented syllables. Lerouchon isn't translating whatever the source of the jubilation is. Suddenly, she yells in French, "You know . . . a French general surrendered . . . He came alone to surrender . . ."

I see Madame Aufresne crying. She told me later that she was crying from shame.

The Germans leave us. They are bringing hay into a kind of cellar. They spread it on the floor and over some barrels. This is our designated refuge for the night.

Soutreux and Lerouchon are speaking German to each other in loud voices. To tell the truth, where there are Germans, they feel too much at home. They are forgetting that they're only guests. A non-commissioned officer brusquely orders them to shut up. He's right, after all.

We lie down on the straw, some of us on the ground, others on the barrels. Toward three in the morning someone declares that the shell impacts are getting closer and that our shelter is far from strong. We dash across fields. Mortar shells are whistling . . . I don't like the sound. But after the jolt caused by the initial explosions, I can't help but ignore the mortars. I manage with great difficulty to overcome the idea that the mortars are not part of my personal universe . . . We don't speak the same language. This game of artillery is as alien to me as the game of belote.

Before reaching Lorris, lying on the grass with a pain in my shoulders while the trucks filed by endlessly, I'd already rediscovered the soldier in me, the soldier of 1915, lost in events. This was only a kind of camping trip that I imagined as temporary. Now, I feel only desolate and numb. Yes, it's as if everything inside me were frozen . . . I rediscover the soul, the torpor and the passions of a soldier. I'm sleepy, I'm hungry and I'm full of certainties. The 1914 war was limited in its goals, modestly territorial, modestly economic. At stake this time is the totality of man, the totality of all men. So vast that to express it, the masses and their masters can no longer come up with token lies. Those conducting this war haven't invented stories of severed hands; neither have the masses.

We reach a farm around which German soldiers are camping. Some refugees are leaving; they have gathered their bundles in a wheelbarrow. Others have settled in. Once they have understood that we're only temporary guests, they welcome us and offer us coffee.

We sleep in the barn until daybreak. I wander through the courtyard. A German soldier comes over to me, speaking to me gently, but I can't manage to understand him. Nevertheless, we seem to agree on the uncomplicated idea that the war is a sad thing, *traurig . . . traurig** . . . Another soldier comes to talk with him. They look furious. It seems the Lerouchon woman has insulted the soldiers. It's hard to believe there have been a disagreement. Or Lerouchon, who earlier was joking coarsely with the Germans, must have ventured some joke that was misunderstood. The two women come back. The

* Sad.

two Germans are "giving them hell." Lerouchon wants to respond, but Soutreux restrains her. All this in the glimmer of dawn. It's as if two girls were being chased out of a guard post.

We leave the farm. The barrage continues, but very listlessly. Soutreux and Lerouchon take fright, turn back and vanish behind a hedge. They know the side paths and the location of their house. We're trying to rejoin them via the main road. That house is not home for us, but for the moment it's our only refuge. The road is lined with woods, and these woods are full of cannons, horses and German soldiers. The soldiers force us to turn back.

We pass a dead horse (it looks as if it were rearing upside down); we pass near the grave of a German soldier. We cross the village of Dampierre. The ground is strewn with the broken stocks of French rifles. We're no longer hearing cannons. We won't hear them again.

We are resting quite a distance from the road on the edge of some woods. The solitude, the silence are such that the war seems far away. But a telephone wire, laid by the Germans, runs along the ground, hidden in the grass. A soldier comes from the roadway. He approaches and hands us a can of monkey meat.*

I felt humiliated. I was the conquered, who receives his food by the conqueror's generosity. Such is war: it imposes gross simplifications, it thinks poorly, it forces poor thinking, in gross categories; it pits nations against each other in an excess of unity that's nothing but insanity; it contrasts victor and vanquished; it eliminates subtle conflicts and replaces them with a fistfight. As big as the fistfight may be, it's only a fistfight. But at the moment nothing can change the fact that this soldier is victory and I am defeat.

It was a French can of monkey meat. "They" had looted it, stolen it . . . That appeased our conscience.

On the road, with a small detachment of German soldiers in front and behind, two Senegalese infantrymen pass by, prisoners, like two handsome black princes escorted by their ungainly white slaves.

We set off again. A hundred meters down the road we discover a house. A game warden was housed here before the evacuation of

* Military slang for corned beef.

the area. It's now inhabited by a young blond giant, his wife and their seven children. The mother is petite and sweet-tempered. The oldest of the children is not yet fourteen. They play on the grass, in the sun, all of them in shorts or bathing suits. They're not the haggard, pitiful refugees that we left the day before. In fact, they did not wind up here by accident. The father knew the area, the house. He chose this refuge.

We ate the canned monkey. And some peas picked from an abandoned garden. They were good people; all they could give us without depriving the children, they gave us . . . Even a little bread, even some salt, even some wine, even some coffee. And good-heartedly. We're five adults. As for the baby, its mother had brought a box of baby cereal and made it some porridge.

A few stray soldiers come to draw water from the well. One asks for a pan from the kitchen, another a spout to tap a barrel of beer. And he tells us in passing that there is *"eine andere Regierung"** in Paris. He's very large, his eyes very small, his eyelids swollen. I understand what he says; it's simple, like the grammar exercises in secondary school: "Yesterday the French killed three German soldiers . . ." But it's impossible for me to grasp whether he is angry, sad or indignant. I have more the feeling that he is reproaching me for a violation of the rules. What a bizarre idea, killing German soldiers!

On the road a hundred meters from us, a regiment is marching, a rectangle on the roadway. If someone said to me, "The road is weeping," I would have believed it. I'm weeping for France, in this landscape I'm unfamiliar with, that I have not learned to love, a flat landscape with too much sky.

For dinner we had a gruel made of sorrel and bits of a loaf of bread found in the woods. We slept on straw in a tin-roofed shack. Throughout the night we heard the rumble of German trucks and raucous commands. Hitler was taking possession of France.

I was asleep, then woke up with a start. I thought it was the sound of machine guns. It was only duck calls. How beautiful duck calls

* Another government.

are! Completely peaceful. I hadn't realized till that point how much I loved duck calls . . . But there is no longer peace on earth. I'm trapped, surrounded, strangled by war and by this peace that will be even more like war than the previous war was. Why, yesterday, did none of us dare go near two pails filled with green beans? Two full pails that the Germans had left in the yard. The dogs ate them.

We spent the following day there. Why? I can hardly say. "To see how things will turn out, because it's more prudent to wait . . ."

Our host, a sometime pharmacist in a small town in the Nord and sometime pharmacist's assistant at a big firm in Paris, more resembles a Quaker than someone who sells ear drops. His philosophy, his politics, I relate without commentary. "France has been punished and deserved it. But England will save itself and save us. Providence will abandon neither France nor England."

He guesses that I don't quite believe in Providence and interrupts his general theme to point out to me more specifically the evidence of divine intervention.

"There are many, it has been proved, who passed through machine-gun fire with a simple little insignificant prayer."

And he resumes his theme of France saved. "France will pick herself up again, because after the war there will no longer be money to pay schoolteachers and members of parliament."

For two days we've been free of the carnival maniac and the lady of the manor with her 4,000-franc windowpanes who guzzles champagne with Germans. And we've felt real relief. Nevertheless, we have to return to her house. It's our only refuge. We cross through a thicket; the sun shines through the branches and the ground is crimson. All this had been protected from the war. For a moment the world can be reduced to the contemplation of this brushwood. I recall that in a trench in 1915, as I was peeling an orange the fruit seemed to me as if it had been protected by its rind from the war, from the filth of the war, as if it were the only pure thing on earth, the only thing the war hadn't touched.

The Germans are occupying the Soutreux woman's house, the fields, the woods toward the Loire, the woods on the other side of the road. The courtyard is full of them.

I repeat to myself stupidly, "I'm no longer in France . . ." It's true that they seem to be at home. The soldiers that we had seen at the mystical pharmacist's house had a certain humane tentativeness, they were alone, tourists lost in the countryside; they weren't filled with the pride of a victorious army. But the ones here are a combat unit. They exhibit a deliberate, contemptuous insolence. Or rather, when passing by they ignore us, they make us insignificant. Or they're trying to offend us, to humiliate us. A *Feldwebel** yells over our heads to his men in pidgin French, "Tomorrow big parade in Paris . . ."

I realize that I had not yet admitted the completeness of the defeat. I was thinking of it like a disease one fears and deep down dismisses as impossible. Each of these Germans is the symptom of a disease whose description we had read about but are suddenly discovering on our skins.

A few soldiers are stretched out on folding chairs, as if showing us the bliss and ease of the victory. Could this be simply the effect of my exasperation? Would French soldiers on maneuvers be different? Less oafish, I think, and less childish. Two soldiers are playing with a ball; another, like a kid, rides a bicycle in circles around the courtyard with incredible perseverance.

Soutreux welcomes us very politely. She was very worried about us, she says. She offers to let us sleep on the straw in one of the bedrooms, the only one not occupied by Germans. We slept, separated from them by a thin wall. In the morning, they leave. There was no commotion of departure. We heard a command; they all got up at once, as if they were marching in close order on parade.

The courtyard is free of them. We breathe. It's as if all of France were rid of them.

Lerouchon's niece comes over to us. "It's boring," she tells us. "Now that they're no longer here, it's too quiet."

I found a piece of German bread in the woods. I was alone. No one saw me. I ate it.

The roads are a mess: there are motorbikes, bicycle wheels, tin

* Technical sergeant.

cans, shirts, undershorts, German magazines. I lean over a strange
box that resembles a toy chest. It's a French military telegraph set.

The two nearest farmhouses have been abandoned by their inhabitants and occupied by the Germans for the last two days. They've
been ransacked, the dresser drawers emptied. Whatever didn't seem
worth carrying off has been dumped on the ground. Underfoot are
a wreath of orange blossoms and some framed photographs. Indignation would be hypocritical here. All soldiers in 1914 saw plun-
dered French farms in areas where only French soldiers had passed
through. This form of looting is an act of soldiers, not only Germans.
Tables and chairs have been carried into the courtyard in front of the
house. On top, empty glasses and bottles, a few sheets of paper and
some pencils. German officers or *Feldwebel* stayed here, made themselves comfortable here . . .

There are rabbits dead in their cages. The hens and cows have not
run away. But they do not move, the hens aren't pecking around and
the cows aren't grazing. Both are strangely immobile . . . Not lying
down, standing; in fact more than immobile, frozen, frozen solid,
stuck to the ground as if to a pedestal; chickens and cows after the
end of the world.

We eat our meals in the courtyard, seated on the running board
of the car. Sometimes an old car becomes a sort of home. Our meals:
a sardine and a little found bread. We are a flying column, gypsies.
But starting the following day, Soutreux brings us or sends her maid
with a pot of soup and a bottle of wine. Her kindness is a little sour,
a little reluctant. We respond with a hypocritical politeness. We fear
above all being thrown out, finding ourselves on the road without
shelter, a road that leads nowhere. We accept without qualms, and
our hypocrisy seems justified to us. The woman who offers champagne to German soldiers can very well, after all, offer us a little soup
without our feeling an excess of gratitude . . . We accept the way prisoners accept their rations. For in Soutreux's house, we are evidently
not in France. We are not exactly in Germany either. We're in a country we didn't know existed: a France that has come to terms with the
German victory, or rejoices in it, a France that feels no connection
to French customs or French character. We looked at this woman

with bewilderment. We didn't understand. And we asked ourselves whether she belonged to the "fifth column."

Doubtless she calculates the price of the food, as she calculates the price of her beveled-glass windowpanes, her gardener's hours and her mattress (it's a 1,200-franc mattress). We are providing our food and part of hers. Neither she nor we will eat her chickens or their eggs. From abandoned farms we bring back everything edible that the Germans left behind. I caught two stray rabbits; one I pinned against a fence, the other I cleverly forced into the corner of a cellar; two nourishing rabbits, two rabbits that are a diplomatic gift.

That is when, for the first time, I heard the word *salvage* used in a new sense that seemed strange to me. For me the word had only an industrial and chemical resonance. I knew, for instance, that by-products are salvaged. But everyone who brought back things found on the road (whether it was a motorcycle or a handkerchief) or looted from abandoned cars said candidly, "Here's what I salvaged . . ."

The *vieux monsieur* salvaged like a magpie. To him everything was good. It was his only occupation and his only concern. He was a true believer. He prowled from Les Douciers to the farms and from the farms to Les Douciers. Nothing escaped his investigations, not a calendar hanging on a wall or a tin of rice powder that had rolled into the roadside ditch. He exhibited his finds like a collector who discovered a magnificent bargain, a rare piece. He's insistently generous. You'd think he worked only for the community. But he hides the big prizes and never offers anything but useless leftovers: for instance, the bottom of a zinc box with a sprinkling of ground coffee and powdered sugar in it. He offers them with a kind of bossy aggressiveness and seems furious if they are disdained.

His son is a more ambitious salvager. He is nowhere to be seen during the day. He drives the roads at the wheel of a luxury car (this car uses more than twenty liters per hundred kilometers) and claims to be engaging in auto repairs. Indeed he is playing the role of the resourceful mechanic with a cigarette in the corner of his mouth. But he returns the first evening with four spare tires, and as he opens his trunk I see three car batteries, clean as polished shoes and without a speck of corrosion on the terminals.

He returns from the roads, roads of misery where women on foot drag exhausted children, and says to me, "It's a gold mine right now, the roads."

If salvaging involves the abolition of a sense of ownership, it also involves its immediate reconstitution. This sense is, if I may say so, salvaged very quickly. The previous day, the Soutreux woman got hold of an abandoned bicycle. The following day she notices that its basket has disappeared. She's outraged and shouts, "My basket has been stolen . . ."

A van transporting office or factory workers has been parked in a field quite far from the road. The driver took this futile precaution hoping his van would be sheltered from looters. Soutreux suggests we "go look" at this van. With complete innocence, she orders her maid to bring a wheelbarrow. We're not the first explorers. There's a pitiful flea market on the grass, which is covered with file folders and administrative papers. And three typewriters catch the rays of the setting sun. In the field these office machines, the black metal and white keys, have a pathetic luster. A sort of exaltation seizes Madame Soutreux. "These machines," she says, "are easily worth two or three thousand francs." She bends down, and the maid goes over to the wheelbarrow.

But all of a sudden a peasant woman herding her cows appears at the edge of the field and screams at us, and there's no talking back: "Get the hell away from here . . . bunch of thieves. Quick . . . This is my place."

Soutreux leads the way with her maid pushing the wheelbarrow. We follow. It's like a funeral procession.

Here the reader shouldn't give in to an overly righteous indignation; he shouldn't judge from the heights of pure morality. I'd like to give a true image of this woman and not distort any trait. Don't judge her the way one would on the Boulevard de la Madeleine in peacetime. When doctors identified kleptomania, they demanded indulgence for the neurotic women who stole in department stores. These women, they said, had been led to steal by the mass of dresses and finery, deprived of their willpower, hypnotized in these palaces of a thousand and one baubles. Here everything is strewn on the road, in the paths, in the fields. Everything seems like abandoned property, on offer: what the Germans left, what the first scavenging refugees left, all of it, from the can of preserves to the typewriter, from the evening dress to the motorcycle. Refugees find and take whatever there is, just as castaways on a desert island have no scruples about grabbing flotsam.

But this excuse doesn't seem valid to me for Soutreux. The reader will judge. In Les Douciers the Germans left some fifty bicycles that they had stolen or looted (whichever you'd prefer) in the Seine-et-Marne and Seine-et-Oise. Soutreux mobilizes us, Aufresne and I. She asks us to haul up and store these bicycles in her hayloft. "I will give them to people from the area when they return . . ." This patriotic philanthropy can only be a lie. There are scarcely five or six isolated farms within a radius of one kilometer. Soutreux could have given a more convincing pretext but she didn't think of it: all the bicycles carry a plate with a name and an address. She could have said, "I'll notify these people . . . that way they'll recover their bicycles after the war."

I admit that we, Aufresne and I, were accomplices in this mass salvaging, this stockpiling. I complied out of weakness, out of obedience to the feudal lord, owner of the land where we were taking shelter, out of false politeness. Anyway, at that moment I didn't realize the obsession with accumulation and the cupidity of our hostess. This filching of bicycles is of little interest, it might be said. We'll see later on that I could not have passed over it in silence.

We left Paris two weeks ago. We're living in a prison, walled in by uncertainties. We have no gasoline; we don't know the general situation or the possibilities of getting around. We're receiving no news.

My son left Paris a few hours before us. He is fifteen and left in a car with two friends, the younger of whom is fourteen and the older not yet eighteen. For more than a month we'll know nothing about them (and thousands are experiencing the same anxiety). Is their car broken down? Have they been machine-gunned? In fact, they were allowed to take the Fontainebleau road and arrived that same evening without problems. But we did not know that.

I open the trunk of the car. I pull out an old blazer of my son's.

That's enough to stir up and intensify the constant anxiety that has taken his place. A garment retains the shape of a person, a shape without foundations or reference points, a shape that is, in a way, immaterial. This presence, this copy, is sometimes unbearable. Because this shape without flesh, which both compels our senses and evades them, which death itself does not destroy, isn't a proof of life.

Bread can now be found in the village of Dampierre, three kilometers from Les Douciers. Soutreux and Lerouchon bring back word from German soldiers. "It's over with France, but not with England . . . A soldier said that." For these women each of these soldiers is a bearer of truth that needs no verification. "A soldier said that."

"The armistice was signed this morning, at five . . ." Soutreux reports.

Lerouchon adds, "The armistice is signed but there's still fighting in the Vosges." They say this as if announcing the start of the hunt. The moment they no longer hear cannons, they no longer feel their destiny connected to events.

I ask, "Who told you that? . . ."

They respond, "A woman on the road." Lerouchon doesn't resent my question. But Soutreux cannot excuse me for it.

"Yes . . . a woman on the road. I'm repeating what she told me . . ." She has some fairly complicated mechanism for loosely comprehending that this unknown woman is not exactly the face of historical truth. But to Soutreux, this truth is verbatim, and my doubt visibly exasperates her.

"The news," the old gardener tells me, "that comes out of the mouth, nobody knows where it comes from." But his wisdom quickly turns into incoherence. At Dampierre a few French refugees' cars were seen driving toward Paris; they flew a white flag. He tells me, "That is a sign that Frenchmen and Germans are equals." I can't get any further explanation from him, and he talks to me at length about a "Frenchman from Gien who was a *Boche* officer."

Soutreux's maid announces peace for the twenty-first of the month. "It was on a parchment that her mother-in-law saw . . ."

A rumor goes around that traffic is unrestricted in the occupied zone but can't pass from the free zone into the occupied zone. So it seems our freedom of movement will extend beyond the occupied zone. An awful way to think, perhaps. But that's what we've come to!

We are waiting. Our thoughts swing from the event to our personal fate, from the heights back to ourselves. A historical panorama is unfolding before me without my being able to do anything about it. The French in 1914 waited, those in 1920 waited. And this collapse: I can only imagine how within a few weeks homegrown moralists will attribute the defeat to abandoning the soil, a taste for ease, disdain for work. It seems to me that France stopped thinking, in the most basic sense of the word. Hypnotized by Hitler or by Stalin, France stopped thinking for itself. When a people don't think twice or no longer think, a Hitler or a Stalin thinks for them. Will the tandem of Hitler and Stalin take over Europe and France with the consent of this sort of Frenchmen, dedicated to a patriotism from newspapers and giving France no face but that of their own complacency?

France always took nourishment from abroad. This assimilating is its whole history since at least the 16th century. But since 1930, part of France, faced with a brutalized Europe, has been in a state of hypnosis; sometimes from admiration, sometimes from horror.

Madame Charroux, who was in tears the other night because in front of the Germans two Frenchmen forgot the dignity of the conquered, is speaking to me today about Communism. Fear of Communism puts her in a trance. But she fears only a word. What she knows about Communism comes from newspapers. She doesn't know that Stalin killed it. And I wonder whether her hatred of the distant Stalin doesn't equal that of the nearby Hitler.

Our current distress momentarily overcomes my self-centeredness.

What is real? The war, politics, man, God? God exists, perhaps, but at more of a distance than religions put him. As he is represented to us, he's an easy answer, good for peace, good for war, good for saints and for common criminals. It makes me think of those all-in-one tools that mechanics disdain—crowbar, pliers, hammer and screwdriver at the same time.

For the moment, the only civilization I've been deprived of is that of matchboxes. Matches are no longer to be found . . . That doesn't bother me. I have a lighter. The childishness of mankind! I'm fond of this lighter and no other. I prefer it out of sentiment. I'm the man with a lighter. I'm a pathetic thing tied to his habits, his quirks, clinging to my pipe and my lighter. My lighter is not just primal fire, the fire of a savage. It's a lighter in a thousand, an amulet, a fetish. If I lost it, I would lose my entire past with it.

I won't go to Ouzouer with my wife to find bread. Thanks to the mayor, who is an old man, and a young baker, the village has bread. But I haven't the strength any longer to go looking for history, the repercussions of history, in a hamlet. I'm waiting for history to come to me. I'm wandering around the courtyard among the cars and the well.

I'm inventing battles, clever strategies. The Germans are allowed to advance as far as the Loire. On the opposite bank, our cannons await. Behind the Germans, our forces advance. The Germans are caught in a crossfire. They try to escape toward their flanks, but our aircraft fly over their lines, ranging between our forward units on the right bank and our artillery on the left bank. Our planes work like plows digging a furrow. Bodies are falling on top of bodies, the same motion as earth turned over by a plowshare. Pleading arms reach toward the sky. They are mowed down. And, no more than a reaper can spare a stalk of wheat once his scythe is swung, our airmen cannot spare the supplicants.

I remake history. Hitler, defeated, is being guarded by a group of sturdy artillerymen, the ones we met outside Lorris who were going to fight at the Loire. Carbines slung over their shoulders, they surround him, this man in a trench coat, a rat in a trap, a rat who can't turn back. An irritable Parisian hurls a "So, little man, it didn't go the way you wanted? . . ." at him. But the others keep their distance and remain impassive: a wall of men surrounding the beast.

Stretched out on the straw with no other view than the plaster on the wall, shutting my eyes to the world like a sick animal, I give myself over to stupid ruminations that have the ease and flow of dreams. Could what we call history be anything more than men's vainest illusions? What we attribute to history in wartime and to the powerful in peacetime, isn't it a sign of our own incapacity? We make history as the sick make sickness. We're responsible for history like the insane are responsible for the creation of asylums.

Maybe Spengler is right. Lucien Febvre quite rightly ranked him, with Count Keyserling, among philosophy's journalists, who made history a thing in itself. Only it is real; men are nothing but empty exteriors. History is God's chessboard. The Germans are playing and winning.

But no . . . nations exist only in their comic-opera aspects, their picturesque qualities, their legends, their books: the Italy of painters, the Spain of dances, the France of Descartes.

A country's characteristics, are they real or fabricated by historians, which is to say, by history's journalists, who are worth no more than the others?

There will always be wars, say those who think in proverbs. But what stupidity to think that war will always be the last resort of history or of men!

I knew the pre-1914 Weimar. Weimar, "capital and residence," which meant that, as capital of the Grand Duchy of Saxony-Weimar-Eisenach, the city had the honor of being the residence of the grand duke. Count Kessler invited me. There we discussed only *Kultur* and *Bildung*.* At the Goethe Archive, old people, or young people who could be mistaken for old people, were studying Goethe's grammar and philosophy. The Nietzsche Archive was a shrine. Nietzsche's sister, Madame Förster-Nietzsche, was keeper of the temple. There I met Professor Andler; bright Viennese; Norwegians, who resembled shepherds; and Swedes, who dressed in Poiret.

The grand duke had "modern" ideas. On the advice of Count Kessler, he had sent for Henri Van de Velde, who, leaving Brussels and giving up Neo-Impressionist painting, devoted himself to rejuvenating architecture and the "minor arts" in the Grand Duchy of Saxony-Weimar-Eisenach. "We don't dress the way we did in the time of Voltaire or Frederick II. We don't want to live in the past like a hermit

* Culture . . . education.

crab. Our houses and our furniture should be our own." Germanic obedience: Van de Velde designed nail heads and the manufacturers of Saxony adopted his models.

Kessler and his friends weren't lying. Nietzsche for them didn't awaken a greater Germany, rather he was a new master of the Ego, a Dionysian Ego as he meant it, an aristocratic Ego gorged on culture. Renoir, Cézanne, Monet, Seurat, Van Gogh were their passwords. They constituted a sort of court modeled on times past, where artists met the world's great men.

Did they have the ulterior motive of world domination? Did they already believe in the historical necessity of a war they didn't want? I wouldn't know how to respond. But even if they believed that only Germany could bring order to the world, that order for them was only the order of external rules, hygiene and transportation networks. France was Greece for them. But, deeply naive, they saw in France only its classic writers and its painters after Watteau. They dreamed of a world whose sole values would be knowledge of the arts and elegant customs. In reality, they didn't just dream of it. They created it, in part. But for themselves alone. An artificial island.

I remember the park, with its stereotypically romantic trees, belonging to the poet Richard Dehmel and Monsieur von Mützenbecher, head of the theater of the Grand Duchy of Baden.

I'm dreaming. My dream erases the years. Monsieur von Mützenbecher appears before me, not in a suit jacket or black morning coat, as I was used to seeing him, but in a German officer's uniform. I turn over on the straw. Monsieur von Mützenbecher is saluting me. I can see that he is surprised by my reserve. These people have hardly any imagination or taste. An oaf like all the others. Does he think I'm going to jump into his arms?

"Weimar," I say to him, "Weimar and Nietzsche and your idolatry of French painting; all that was only a fifth column."

"No," he responds, "the German aristocracy never loved Hitler."

"But it serves him."

"No, it serves Germany. Even if Germany is wrong, even if Germany is criminal; did you want us to betray her? We are not in the

days when generals committed treason without dishonoring themselves. You must admit, that is one of the effects of your democracy . . .
Thus we, the officers, have been obligated to follow our troops. It is
history turned upside down."

He bursts out laughing, a false laughter, a philosophical laughter.

"This is the world inverted, like a glove turned inside out. But our
meeting is the spark, the spark that rights the world . . . Look . . ."

And indeed I see German soldiers forming up, leaving, marching
in step toward the Rhine, returning home.

I no longer saw the Loire. The Loire was no longer anything more
to me than a strategic myth. From the courtyard I see shrubs, fields.
I have no connection to this featureless, flat landscape, which seems
laid out by chance and to which only chance has led me. And I sense
clearly that I'm granted these two meters of courtyard and the straw
I have for the night only reluctantly. Such as when I apologized to
Soutreux for whatever trouble I might cause her, and she replied,
"But no . . . you can certainly stay here for a day or two." Other landscapes, old homesteads, I yearn for them, I can't let go; I'd like to
be there in the blink of an eye, by a miracle. I've left pieces of my
life there. Such as my cousin Nicot's house overlooking the Saône.
How nicely it all comes together: the river, the old gate, the ancient
garden, the welcome and hospitality, the ten-year-old Chardonnay
rich as hazelnuts, the 1840 folding screen that instantly puts me into
a fairy tale. The house in Saint-Amour, the house in Villars, I've
thought about them the way thinking of fruit makes one's mouth
water.

I'd like to escape, to escape to any time, any place where I don't
know the price of mattresses, of beveled-glass windowpanes and
gardeners' hours. I hope to console myself contemplating three
rosebushes against a background of locust trees. It's a momentary
pleasure. An old habit. Man isn't only an eye. These are the war's
roses, the debacle's roses, Soutreux's roses.

Some German planes pass overhead, practically hedge-hopping.
We're watched even from the sky.

A rumor circulates that the Italians are in Nice. At that point
I didn't know I possessed Nice. I didn't know I was the owner of

Nice . . . I didn't realize all my proprietary instincts. Nice had just been snatched away from me.

The *vieux monsieur* comes over to me looking desperate and furious.

"I had salvaged a jar of red-currant preserves . . . The Germans took it."

Aufresne is washing and polishing his unusable car, which has a leaky piston rod. He prunes a hedge. He knows how to kill a rabbit and turn its skin inside out like a glove. He rakes the courtyard. Not just to make himself useful and to please Soutreux. This department-store department manager turned proprietor has remained rustic and a do-it-yourselfer. Just as leisure soothes my boredom, activity relieves his.

He contemplated the words of the Quaker pharmacist. "That man is right," he said, "England will save us . . . England has mastery of the seas; Germany will be able to do nothing against a blockade organized by England."

This is how he translated the mystical pharmacist's providential dogma into economic terms. France had been taken, but he had the English fleet and was launching it across the seas.

I'm not mocking him. Such an emotional reaction doesn't seem ridiculous to me. But I don't know how to juggle mastery of the seas.

A bond has been established between the Aufresnes and us because like us they endure uncomfortably Soutreux's hospitality, her on-and-off congeniality and hostile silence; because like us they feel the baseness of her reverse nationalism in the victors' presence; and because like us they were ashamed by the indecent welcome she gave the German soldiers.

What a place, what circumstances for striking up a friendship! But beautiful friendships aren't born by accident, even the most pathetic of accidents. They are prepared before the first encounter, via separate pathways. And the impact of that encounter isn't for everybody.

I had some difficulty keeping up a conversation with Aufresne.

His kind of bourgeois knows only how to talk about business. I'm not saying he'd lost his soul; he no longer had the language to express it.

Corot's father sold cloth. But he didn't own an automobile and the political issues facing him were not international. And in Corot's father's time the newspapers still had an artisanal character: they weren't yet mass-producing news and doctrine. The difference between articles in the *Constitutionnel* and articles in a newspaper today is the difference between a bolt-action breechloader and a machine gun.

Aufresne mulls over more ideas than a peasant, but a peasant knows much better how to weigh an idea and distinguish what is concrete in it and what is beyond knowing.

Once I was told, "The Dutch peasant is superior to the Belgian peasant because he has read at least one book: the Bible." The descendants of Corot's father in the France of 1940 hadn't read a book, I mean a real book. They read newspapers and magazines. They think in captions and snapshots. This is apparent when they touch on problems of any breadth, politics in particular. Deep down they feel everything escapes them, but they don't admit it. Then they force themselves to give shape to vague ideas, to feelings they've been fed. They personalize them, manipulating France or Britain like marionettes; they gesticulate, raise their voices, it's as if all the muscles in their bodies are working, as if some towering rage or unknown despair is animating them: they want to create truth out of nothingness. When I hear my contemporaries deal with politics I often think about the madwoman in La Salpêtrière who believed the world did not exist beyond what she created, minute by minute. And "squatters" is what she called the chaotic beings she assembled to make the world and "supplement the diligence of the gods," much like our contemporaries vainly assemble "squatters" in politics.

In the same way, Aufresne, who is the calmest of men, is agitated by history. He fears the workers of Belleville and Billancourt. If they're at work, won't they revolt? Who will keep them in line?

"We need to wait," he tells me. "It's better not to return to Paris for a few days . . . not before food supplies have been organized. They can't let us die of hunger . . ."

I recall he intended "they" to mean the French government. We didn't think the Germans' stay in Paris could last more than a few days.

At the crossroads of a byway and the Gien road, two women and two children were resting. They were coming from the Paris area pushing a cart loaded with a trunk and two suitcases. Their clothes were neat and brushed, their faces washed and fresh-looking. As I pointed this out with admiration, one of the women said to me, smiling, "But it's perfectly normal . . . water and straw can be found everywhere."

When the Germans were camping at Les Douciers, Lerouchon held a salon in front of her trailer. A couple of soldiers balanced on folding stools. We could hear peals of laughter.

Behind the house, we opened a can of food (we got a little bread from Ouzouer and Soutreux brought us some soup). Lerouchon came from her trailer offering us three pieces of rabbit. "You're welcome to it, I swear . . ." My wife, thanking her, refused, saying we had enough to eat. I confess, I admire that dignity and regret the rabbit. Something of the soldier was reconstituted in me. I truly believe I would have accepted, for I have been hungry for days and hiding it heroically. And Lerouchon has such an air of a camp follower offering a bottle. So much a camp follower that she doesn't distinguish between French soldiers and German soldiers. It's an air she has. I don't believe her husband, who is at the front, would have anything else to reproach her for. Anyway she speaks of him readily. "Let's hope nothing has happened to him . . . No, I'm sure nothing has . . . I can sense it . . ." She repeats several times, "I sense it . . . I sense it . . . I sense it . . ." And you might say she senses it with her nose: She juts forward a muzzle that grimaces and sniffs.

She has a battery-powered radio in her trailer. We listen to the German broadcast from Compiègne. Chancellor Hitler . . . the rail

car . . . the 1918 monument* . . . No commentary. It's sober and terrible. It's nighttime and a cow is mooing in the meadow.

Radio-Journal de France announces that a prefect who deserted
has been dismissed and that there is fighting on the front in the
Vosges and near Clermont-Ferrand.

I must look unhappy, because Lerouchon bursts out laughing,
shouting in my ear.

"But laugh a little . . ."

What's more, she reassures us about the fate of France.

"It will be a protectorate, like Morocco . . . We won't be any un-
happier; we'll work like before . . ."

Lerouchon is a simple monster. Soutreux is more complicated.
She isn't plebeian, but rather a "*petite dame*," simpering, precious
and pretentious. Lerouchon ties herself into knots; Soutreux more
does somersaults. I'm not searching for the origins of the German
salient these two women set up in the Loiret. I only wish to describe
Soutreux as I saw her day by day, kind or contemptible, hateful or
ridiculous; like a domesticated animal, closer to a dog or cat than a
human being. She differed from the Lerouchon woman in that she
did not express emotions in simple barks; she used a few twigs, a few
slivers of ideas. She told us about a conversation between two Germans. One said that he believed in God but not the God of religions.
Lerouchon would be incapable of retaining and repeating such lofty
abstractions.

Soutreux's husband—I get these details from Aufresne—is of very
humble origins. An industrialist, he owns millions' worth of mer-
chandise in inventory. He is not a talkative man, but his steadiness
and loyalty are certain. I can easily imagine this businessman, who
is not the kind that collects paintings, who absolutely doesn't give
a damn about Jouvet's stage directing, who though a "naturalized"
bourgeois endures not knowing the rites of high society and takes
pleasure in nothing more than hunting and fishing on the weekend.

---

* On June 22, 1940, France signed an armistice dictated by Germany. On Hitler's orders, the signing took place in the same rail car—jackhammered out of a
local monument—and at the same location, near Compiègne, where Germany
had signed the armistice ending World War I.

Does he know his wife's feelings and how she behaves? It can be assumed he disregards women's opinions, particularly his wife's. Soutreux herself told us he spends whole days around her without speaking. But the simplest prudence or most basic decency would have led him to restrain his wife from showing herself to be so scandalously German.

This taste for Germany is her distinguishing trait. Other than that, she is maternal with dogs. She is escorted by a group of yelping beasts, and this barking seems to delight her. They sleep in her bed. I admit I don't like the foxhound much. She bends over him tenderly, murmuring gently, "Where is my little professor?" and the foxhound instantly howls as if at the moon without ever having to be coaxed. She has pity for the rabbit she'll eat tomorrow and says "poor little animal" to it with touching warmth. She is sympathetic toward stray dogs, and God only knows how many are wandering about. But she grumbles if her butane or firewood is used to cook the baby's cereal. To make it, the Aufresnes build a fire in the meadow.

She's as childish as a fifty-year-old girl, and if she tries to be imposing, she has the gravitas of a teacher's aide on holiday.

She's a little bohemian but not ugly, though she has thick arms and legs. She speaks French without an accent but is said to have been born in central Europe and to have relatives in Vienna. But I don't see that, at any rate, as an excuse. As a foreigner married to a Frenchman, she might speak discreetly out of normal decency, if not prudence.

Her linguistic mistakes aren't those of a foreigner, though. She gives words ambiguous meanings, like people who will never speak a language fluently, even their own. Wanting to show admiration for a politician to whom she attributes a great knowledge of foreign customs, she says, "He is very international." But she has what language teachers call a vocabulary. She aspires to conversation and speaks to me with disdain about people who aren't cultivated. Perhaps the only time in two weeks that I wanted to laugh was when I heard that word from her mouth.

"A German colonel," she tells us with a hint of pride, "asked me for a private conversation . . . He told me France had been overfond of ease but that she would pick herself up again. He told me that by his own hand he had killed twelve Senegalese prisoners, who for him are less than dogs . . ."

She pauses for a while, then continues in a quasi-confidential tone.

"What he wanted was information about Frenchmen's state of mind . . ."

You see this scene in novels or onstage at the theater: the Frenchwoman, with all her finesse, disarming and disconcerting the barbarian. But Soutreux has no background in theater.

We often wondered whether Lerouchon and Soutreux were part of the fifth column. It always seemed unlikely to me. It's inconceivable that a traitor would not feign perfect loyalty while in the country he's betraying. The shamelessness, the insolence of Lerouchon and Soutreux stunned me. They were inexplicable to me then. Moreover, it doesn't seem to me that propaganda for the enemy that was so overt and so crude would be effective. Today I believe the crazed lip service for order, even Hitler's order, that came over part of conquered France had infected these dull souls.

When the Germans had left Les Douciers and their nearest billet was three kilometers away in the village of Dampierre, one of their trucks turned off the road and came into the courtyard. Soutreux rushed over to the cab, occupied by the driver and a noncommissioned officer. A conversation began that I didn't understand. It was evident that the noncommissioned officer did not come under orders but for a visit. He had enormous, very white teeth. Soutreux was beaming, smiling, happy, though nothing led me to believe her happiness was anything more than speaking in German about Germany with a German.

But the following is more suspect. Two horse carts had stopped in front of the house: some peasants who had fled on the announcement of the German advance and been unable to cross the Loire at Gien had turned around and were coming back home.

"I told you not to leave," Soutreux shouted at them, "that the Germans would do you no harm . . . but that those who did not return quickly would not be allowed to move back in . . ."

The armistice had not been signed. We had no news except what circulated by word of mouth and was born out of thin air by spontaneous generation. That the Soutreux woman might claim several days before the Germans' arrival that they would do no harm is explainable: to the extent that someone can love a group, a people, she loved them; for her their arrival was a blessing. Her certainty of a German victory, of their advance to the Loire, is explainable as well: she considered them invincible. But how could she have foreseen that the Germans would distinguish between abandoned farms and those that peasants had temporarily evacuated? She was wrong only on a detail. The Germans indeed ransacked only abandoned houses in this region, but they were not opposed to the return of peasants who had fled. But that's thinking like a prosecutor.

In Dampierre, Soutreux met with a woman I know nothing about except that local people whisper that she is a "fifth columnist." She speaks German volubly, giddily, ostentatiously. What to conclude? Except that during the last war I knew how to laugh at spies' disguises. I truly believe Soutreux loved Germany with an exhibitionist passion.

Some attribute to young women a sentimental pity for soldiers. I think Lerouchon might have welcomed French soldiers as willingly as she did German soldiers. It wasn't the same with Soutreux. This proves it.

On the path in front of the house is an example of those one-of-a-kind, homemade carts that before the exodus would have been ashamed to be on the highway. Next to it three young men are resting, wiping their brows. They are three French soldiers from the Forty-Sixth or Forty-Seventh Division. Taken prisoner by the Germans, they escaped. Two of them had been captured twice and twice had escaped. They have formed a band; they have linked their fates. One of them is from the Nièvre, the other two from the Jura. They were given civilian clothes, and they got rid of all their identity papers. They're navigating by the sun and a map, avoiding the highways, taking small roads. They'd fought at the Somme. Their morale had been good. They might have held on had they seen French aircraft and been given ammunition. "Then," they said, "we understood . . . The order was, every man for himself . . ."

They left like the rest, southward. They met a motorcyclist who told them, "Don't worry . . . they're twenty-five kilometers behind you . . ." The motorcyclist, who spoke perfect French, dashed off ahead of them. Half an hour later they found German soldiers barring their route.

One of them is a railway worker, the other a farmer, the third a cheese maker in Lons-le-Saulnier. They were undaunted by fatigue, they had already gone about a hundred kilometers. Another hundred kilometers for the railwayman to be home. The two others must walk another three hundred kilometers.

It must be said, Soutreux brought the three French soldiers a bottle of wine. But I don't count the generosity of this gift for much, because I remember the champagne she offered the Germans. Not that I prefer sparkling wines, not at all! But I know the hierarchy of wines, to the extent Soutreux can provide them.

Experienced walkers, the three soldiers mixed their wine with plenty of water from the fountain. They were about to set off again, pushing their cart, which contained some food and three travel bags. They were about to set off and we were thinking of the fifty bicycles that Soutreux had stored in her hayloft. We were thinking of them, but she wasn't. I still reproach myself to this day for not having been imperious and rude. I was a coward. It was my wife who made a discreet allusion to the stock of bicycles, which Soutreux chose not to understand. That was too much. We signaled to the three soldiers and went to fetch three bicycles. They fastened the straps of their bags to their shoulders, straddled the bicycles and disappeared.

I don't know what became of the soldiers, but Soutreux never forgave us.

I bathe in the Loire, a miserable bath. It's more a soap and rinse. I'm returning to Les Douciers by way of the fields. I hear a call. I see a Senegalese infantryman appear on the riverbank, like a god emerging from the water.

He had been hiding in the woods, or rather in the thicket. What help can I give him? Soutreux would not take him in. And though I don't have the right to accuse her of being connected to the Germans other than by friendship, I suspect she's capable of inflating her importance and showing them her consideration by handing over this

Negro. I can't even think of getting him into some civilian clothes: he's black.

His stature, his gait have an elegance that whites rarely have, the elegance of deer and gazelles. It's a bit silly and straight out of Larousse, but I think of how the goddess is revealed by her gait. What naive charm in that innocent smile! He smiles while talking to me, he's smiling under the threat of capture or death, as if his eyes were playing with the landscape, playing with me, as if despite the war there was a magic in the world that made him smile. I remember the Senegalese whom Lucie Cousturier introduced me to in Fréjus and a certain Amadou Lo, who wrote Lucie a letter that ended: "I say hello to everything in the house and in the garden." I'm also thinking about the German colonel who Soutreux claimed killed them by the dozen.

What can I do for him? I advise him not to go back up to Les Douciers; I tell him the Germans are in Dampierre and suggest he keep hidden in the underbrush. There's some on an islet in the middle of the Loire that can be reached by a ford. I believe if he can hold out for three or four days, chances are he will not be shot. Indeed, in the area they talk of little else besides the armistice and the imminent peace. What's more, the two terms are often confused, sometimes I learn that the armistice had been signed at four in the morning, sometimes I hear it will be tomorrow. But my Senegalese will need something to eat. He pulls four cans of monkey meat from his haversack to show me.

I ask him how he eluded the Germans. The story he tells me is so astonishing and so full of hope that I had him repeat it so I could check it with questions and cross-references (one Jesus Christ is enough . . .).

He was wandering in the woods. He saw a German leaning against a tree. The German signaled him to approach. "Me *thought* he was goin' to *kill* me . . ." The German gave him four cans of monkey and said, "Beat it; you're on your own . . ."

He rummages through his haversack again and offers me a pack of cigarettes. It wasn't to curry favor. I had shaken his hand and we were about to separate. It was a magnificent gift, like in legendary times.

The armistice, the peace . . . "You have to count on about a week, perhaps two, between the armistice and the peace. The roads are open . . . but only in the direction of Paris . . . The Germans want everyone to return to Paris." Bells are rung in Dampierre, it's the armistice; other bells, it's the peace. "The occupation cannot last a long time . . . But they will demand an enormous sum . . ."

I know that the road is open as far as Gien; I know nothing more. I wander idly around Soutreux's yard. We are looking for another house, a room, a barn. But the farmhouses are quite far from one another and, mysteriously, more concealed in this flat countryside than anywhere else. In the meantime, the Soutreux woman invites us to stay a few more days. She offers us a mattress, a beautiful mattress, she tells us. She invites us to her table. I'm very happy to sit at a table. It's a highly civilized luxury that I've lost the habit of. But mealtimes are trying nonetheless. We and the Aufresnes maintain a prudent silence that makes for a heavy atmosphere.

The *vieux monsieur* went back to Paris with his son. But before leaving he told us that Soutreux had confided to him that the Aufresnes were being very tactless by settling in with her. This is a delicate way of making us feel that we ourselves . . . He did not seem at all pleased by our presence. Doubtless he was afraid we were competitors in salvaging. He repeated insistently, while Soutreux insinuated discreetly, that the difficulties of driving on the roads were much exaggerated. To hear them, it was like driving on a racetrack. There were greased roadways where French municipalities and the German *Kommandanturs** were fighting over who could distribute the most bread and gasoline.

The worst is that Soutreux is not at all being cruel about this. She's poorly suppressing very natural feelings that a more polished soul might reject or transform. I feel strongly that if I had to lodge strangers in my home, where I seek solitude, where I want only proven friends, I would hardly feel an irresistible joy. I would not give in to the ancient laws of hospitality or Franciscan tradition with instant enthusiasm. But the slightest human spark on the part of the

* Headquarters.

unknown guests would make me forget that my sanctum was being violated. And we're not living in ordinary times. History is being mass-produced for us. Soutreux couldn't sense that any more than Lerouchon. History passes over them as over beasts. We are shipwrecked. Soutreux sees us only as importunate.

If Soutreux's house were one of those old homes where the objects and furniture have the aura of relics, it would be understandable that she suffered by bringing in strangers. But she's putting us in empty rooms where the bare plaster is still fresh. The most surprising is that in sheltering the Aufresnes and us she seems to be resigning herself to some noble sacrifice, but when lodging a detachment of Germans, who turned her house into a barracks, she welcomed them the way Biblical patriarchs welcomed guests. Even the empty food cans they scattered in her garden did not put this meticulous housekeeper in a bad mood.

All this led us to some ignoble thoughts that I must recall here. The circumstances are such that even begging would seem barely less humiliating to us. But the Aufresnes, like us, don't want to be indebted to Soutreux for anything but the space in her courtyard and her empty rooms. We don't want her bread. We fetch bread in Dampierre. Two or three kilometers from Les Douciers some isolated farmhouses are newly reoccupied by their owners, who were unable to cross the Loire. There we buy some chickens and some eggs, which feed us and Soutreux.

That's how we explore the countryside. We pass a shack in whose doorway stands an old woman leaning on a stick; she remains still except for her head, which is trembling. We weren't able to tell whether the house was hers or not. She says nothing to us but, "I's walked . . . I's walked."

At the first farm we reach, the people have just returned. They have come back with a very agitated strapping young man about whom I could gather only two things: that he is Parisian and that his forearms are covered with tattoos. I don't recall whether he was one of their relatives or an unknown refugee. I won't repeat all his remarks, which express the total resignation that follows panic among some Frenchmen because they have discovered its brutal oscillations between fear and the illusion of security. These people were afraid that the Germans casually kill everyone. They survived. They were relieved and didn't even know whether they were hopeless or happy. The young man does not recount his flight, his personal adventure, easily. There's surprise and anger in his words. "In Ouzouer, there were Germans . . . They gave us a room." (He doesn't add that the village was nearly empty then and the Germans few in number.) "They gave us a room and something to eat midday and evening . . . The French didn't do as much."

We go as far as another farm. The farmers had left and then returned before the departure of the Germans, who had looted savagely. But the wife had been able to save her horse, which the Germans wanted to take.

"They took my husband's shirts from us," she says, "our clothing . . . When we came back, I killed a duck and cooked it. When it was cooked, a German seized it and ate it by himself, in front of me . . . It was an officer who slept in my room. Look what they did . . . they tore spikes out of the stable and nailed them here (she shows me the bedroom wall) . . . to hang the officer's uniform."

In another corner of the room, the flowered wallpaper had been torn. It's a little thing, but there's an ownership that's solely from the heart. This peasant woman was as distressed and hurt by this torn wallpaper as by the hole in the roof of her stable from a mortar.

We find Soutreux contemplating her butane stove melancholically. "I would have enough for myself alone," she says. "But my supply isn't inexhaustible . . . To use the gas for so many people, soon I won't have any more . . . What will I do then? . . ."

She's not speaking to us; she's not speaking to the Aufresnes. She seems to be unaware of our presence. She's appealing to the stove, apparently.

We deliberate with the Aufresnes. Lerouchon has agreed to let me have a few liters of gasoline. I have enough to go about fifty kilometers. Aufresne, as I've already said, is immobilized by a leaky piston rod. He would like me to tow him. I hope he knows I would have done it willingly if my clutch had allowed.

Where to find refuge? Which roads are open and in what direc-

...rotting in ditches, its hungry and desperate families and those who preyed on them, its defeated and demobilized French soldiers, and, soon, the exultant Germans, swooping through their conquered lands.

Werth and his wife soon run out of petrol. They find refuge first with a woman who loves Germany with an "exhibitionist passion", and whose "dull soul had been infected by a crazed lip service to order, even Hitler's order". Escaping her hateful company, they are taken in by a generous farmer and his wife, but must soon share the farm with changing platoons of German soldiers – big, blond men, "death's heads topped with flax". Long before France was ensnared in "le temps des autruches" ("the time of ostriches") – the complicated game between occupiers and occupied – Werth was writing of their troubled relations with delicacy.

Saint-Exupéry, younger than Werth by twenty-two years, regarded his friend as his literary mentor. His "Letter" is an elegy to their friendship, to France, to his roots. Werth survived the war in a small village in the Jura, where he was indeed hungry. Saint-Exupéry did not. His plane disappeared while on a reconnaissance mission over the Mediterranean in July 1944. *33 Days*, admirably translated by Austin Denis Johnston, is a beautifully written portrait not just of the shock of sudden occupation, but an eloquent essay on the meaning of how to remain human, even in the face of such confusing adversity.

CAROLINE MOOREHEAD

and continually to the gloom of the New
the alternative assessment of English stability
was once very common, and that is, as it were,
here are the tones of a resolute Whiggism that
tive fitness of one another". What one hears
selective affinity" that "enhance the reproduc-
evident
English
of pro-
persua-
e mode
erty".
, in all
"self-
ges in
t the
seen
n to
. In
cer-
ne

Léon Werth
33 DAYS
Translated by Austin D. Johnston
144pp. Melville House. Paperback, $16.
978 1 61219 425 7

"He lives in France, where he is hungry and cold", wrote Antoine de Saint-Exupéry in his dedication of *Le Petit Prince* to his "best" friend, the Jewish writer and art critic Léon Werth (1878–1955). "He needs to be comforted." Werth was then trapped in German-occupied France; Saint-Exupéry had made it to the United States. The two men never saw each other again. For the first time, Werth's short book on "l'exode", the flight south of some 8 million French people in the early summer of 1940, has been brought together with the introduction that Saint-Exupéry wrote for it, "Letter to a Friend", both texts at various points lost.

Much has been published in recent years (not least works by Irène Némirovsky) on the great exodus of cars, horse-drawn carts, prams, wheelbarrows, vans and bicycles that flowed south from Paris towards the Loire. *33 Days*, which Werth wrote while in hiding, is a remarkably vivid description of this chaotic river, its vehicles abandoned by the roadside, its dead horses rotting in ditches

tion? We have friends in the Yonne, but hadn't they fled? We decide to go to Chapelon: We'll ask Abel Delaveau for shelter. Even if Soutreux hadn't by unsubtle hints made us feel the weight of her limited hospitality, we could not have stayed: We were infuriated by the revolting atmosphere at Les Douciers, by the human stink one breathes there, we could no longer stand Soutreux's pinched hysteria or Lerouchon's low-class hysteria. In our shipwreck, Abel Delaveau's farm seems a happy island to us. But has Abel Delaveau returned home? Is he stuck, with his horse carts, short of Gien or beyond Gien? Who can know? But we're no longer hesitating. We're playing our luck. It's too late to leave this evening. We'll leave tomorrow morning.

I informed Soutreux of my decision. Her expression was sour and sniveling at the same time. I'm well aware of her grievances. She can't forgive us the three bicycles that she didn't dare refuse but which are now missing from her stockpile. I'm not accusing her of being selfish; I believe her inspiration is the commercial valuation of objects and that she's in the grip of an unselfish obsession with collecting, with accumulating. She can't forgive us our polite sarcasms either. She doesn't have as thick a skin as Lerouchon. Accustomed to ruling over her maid and a crowd no doubt dazzled by her 4,000-franc windowpanes, she sensed our resistance, our distaste. She could not analyze her unease. Like the insane, whose delirium is only a rational justification of their anguish, she looked for its causes. She found absurd, childish ones, but nothing she considered beneath her.

"Monsieur," she says, "I really do not know if I can invite you to my table anymore. Yesterday your wife gravely insulted me . . . She was the one to carve the chicken . . . And to whom did she first pass the platter? Whom did she serve first? . . . Me? . . . No, monsieur . . . Am I not the mistress of the house? . . . Isn't the plate offered first to the person of honor? . . ."

I would like the reader to excuse me for recounting this harangue. But I'm not writing a novel and I can't choose my characters. Besides, the stupidity of even this woman, in contrast, at a time like this, had a kind of pathos. And this woman, whose presence in normal times we might have ignored to begin with, we had been her guests, and in our distress we had come to her carried away with premature gratitude.

Whether she invented this grievance or she believed it, I saw a form of vanity, or rather oversensitivity, that I've seen only in the lowest-class girls, and even then only when they're cooped up.

As for the rest, I'm leaving out only the two or three responses with which I tried, dispassionately, with the impassiveness of a clinician, to slow her monologue. I'm reporting her words unchanged, like a psychiatrist records the words of a patient.

Soutreux was now moving on to a more realistic complaint.

"I'm treated like a *Boche* . . . I don't care. I know very well that it displeased you that I speak German . . . a certain jealousy perhaps . . ."

Then she tells the beads of a rosary of litanic clichés typical of an old biddy.

"I'm a simple woman, monsieur . . . But, without knowing your means, mine are perhaps greater than yours. I don't know what education your wife has received, perhaps I have more . . . Your wife's cast of mind is not mine . . . Still, there are some who came here and left with tears in their eyes. I regret . . . monsieur . . . I would have liked to chat with you about your writing . . . but in my house I do as I please, and what is essential is for me to get along well with my husband . . ."

This wording seems revealing to me, I won't comment on it . . .

Forgive me, Saint-Ex; forgive me, Tonio. You wouldn't recount such mediocrities. You delete or burn them. You make crystal. But I don't know how to fly. At the moment, I'm touching down in lowly places. I no longer expect much from myself or the world. I'm old when you're not around. Where are you? I don't even know if you're alive. I dream sometimes that your airplane had been hit, that it crashed in a catastrophe of scrap metal and fire. I drag myself along in my old métier. I recount the lowly; I tell, in the immensity of this war, the stories of insects.

So that evening we became gypsies, a flying column again, in a corner of the courtyard. The Aufresnes brought us soup. My wife didn't want to touch it, even though the broth was made from our chicken. But Madame Aufresne insisted so gently that we completely disregarded whatever opinion Soutreux would have of us. Those who have never been nomads on the roads in a disaster will say, of what interest is the soup? The Aufresnes truly proved here that they had nobility and courage. Their fate depended on the Soutreux woman. A little cowardice . . . they might have distanced themselves from us. They did not do so. And when they'd had dinner with Soutreux, they came to chat with us a moment longer.

IV

CHAPELON UNDER THE BOOT

We drive toward Chapelon. On the road we pass only a few cars, which are transporting German officers. They are French makes, and the Germans have painted them dark gray. We see the dead horses again, the horses from the battle scenes. But their bellies are swollen and they give off a stench.

We again pass through the places where we were witnesses of a battle in miniature; where some French artillerymen surrendered and where others, under fire, tried to get a caisson back on the roadway from the roadside ditch; where an artillery horse crashed down on the fender of our car. This landscape had been distorted by battle, noise, violence and danger. It had all been there: helmeted Germans, French artillerymen cut off from their units, frightened civilians, horses rearing, horses down, horses upside down. But the battlefield and this landscape were separated as if by a frame, with a little sky on top. Our memory can't find its place in these empty spaces, where a few accordioned cars seem to have been swept into the roadside ditch and evoke nothing more than an accident, a collision. The road, the fields, the woods, the house are no more than topography. A farmhouse on the near side of the road, a flat expanse, that's all.

"The opposite of childhood memories," my wife says. "The gardens we thought were enormous seem minuscule. Here, everything is empty and more vast than we thought."

What will Abel Delaveau's farm be like? Untouched? Ransacked?

Has he returned? How sad if I find the farm abandoned or Abel Dela-veau in an empty house, his barn without cows, his stables without horses.

Everything is intact. Abel Delaveau and his carts took the same route we did. But he turned around after two days on the road.

I'll say nothing about your welcome, Abel Delaveau. Many years ago, I nearly drowned in the ocean. When I felt land under my feet, it was as if I'd been reborn into a new life. Seeing you again, I feel the same safety. Being back with you, I find a human quality again, which is indispensable for me and which I'd been deprived of since the night when, at the same time as you, I left Chapelon. I'm relieved. I can worry, feel sadness, but no longer despair. It seemed as if you expected us. So much so that it seemed completely natural to have come to ask you for shelter, you whom I still barely knew. There was no false effusiveness between us. You and your wife were simple, as simple as I'd like to be. I'm about to offend you perhaps; I know you are touchy on the subject of peasants. You have a certain peasant pride. Well, I tell you this . . . the idea, widespread in cities, that peas-ants always have a patriarchal simplicity is false. Above all, I know peasant women whose manners are as affected as city women's. Sim-plicity is not the privilege of a single class, even the peasant's. I was your guest; I'm not thanking you. One gives thanks for a present, or even a kindness, but not for a fraternal gift.

Your wife takes us to the bedroom where we had slept for a few hours. The mantel is decorated with a clock, two candelabras and a framed photograph under glass: It is you, in a frock coat, with your wife on your wedding day, holding hands. It's only a photograph, and an old-fashioned one, but it has the charm of an old song.

We are no longer tourists separated from a caravan, which was still rolling along in the unoccupied territories. We are no longer transient guests. We are prisoners of a sort. We have no more gaso-line at all and don't yet know the conqueror's wishes with regard to road travel.

Because of the farm work, we'd be a nuisance for Madame Dela-veau if we ate at her table. We'll board with Madame Rose, the wife of a road mender who was called up; she lives with her daughter and son in a house a hundred meters from the farm. When I came back from the Far East, it wasn't a shock to return to Marseille and France. But coming from Les Douciers to Chapelon, I truly had the feeling of a homeland regained, a feeling strong enough to be mixed with surprise. I don't know how we would have endured had we been prisoners in Germany. At Soutreux's we endured an atmosphere of ambiguity, where anyone who showed sorrow for France's defeat was suspect. While eating the soup prepared by Madame Rose, I want to scream, "I'm in France . . ."

I would discover later that Abel had left with his horse carts and his two cars in tow. Besides his family, he took Madame Rose, her daughter and an old man and his wife who were dragging themselves along, having set out on foot. Near Lorris, because aircraft were straf-ing, they took shelter in a ditch. An old peasant remained sitting on the road, dangling his legs in the ditch. He was exposing himself to machine-gun fire and bomb shrapnel. He had reached the limit of despair. Abel urged him to take cover. "No," the old man said, "it'll be better if I'm hit, it'll be over."

While Abel is sheltering his caravan in some woods, the Germans cross through the same woods . . . The women are worried. Abel reas-sures them. "Give me a break! Can't you see these are Englishmen?"

The Germans had only passed through Chapelon. Here are a few remarks reported by Madame Rose and that I didn't confirm. Some soldiers entered an evacuated farmhouse and emptied all the draw-ers. They took watches and jewelry. Elsewhere, they slapped and hit a woman who was alone in her house, forcing her to show them where she had hidden her money. They took 3,000 francs. The woman, or another one, complained to an officer, who said to her, "This is war . . . Do you take care of our dead? . . ." After the armistice was signed, the Germans danced all night in Ladon. And two women from the town, who had not previously been "loose," danced with them; this even though in Ladon itself they had shot thirteen French soldiers and eight civilians.

We had only one day without Germans. The next day, they were in the village.

It was after dinner. Two soldiers came in. They were looking for bedrooms. Madame Rose told them her house is small and she has no beds other than hers and the children's. But one of the soldiers put his hand on the doorknob of the door between the kitchen and bedrooms.

"I want to see (*I vant to zee*) . . . ," he said.

We knew we were "under the boot," but at that moment we felt it inside our skins.

They looked through the house and left without saying anything, without even looking at us.

I don't need a dictionary to describe the difference between force and authority. I'm nothing more than a member of a captive tribe.

They're next to us, up against us and all around us. They're outside the house and inside the house, which they enter whenever they like.

The peasants are more shocked than we are to see them now wandering around nearly naked except for shorts or even bathing suits that look like old-fashioned pajamas. A strong movie culture has accustomed us to such collective nudism. Onscreen, that's how people procreate. But the Germans aren't naked only for gymnastics and aerobic exercises. They're naked all the time, naked to eat, naked to clean their rifles, naked to smoke. They're naked and they yell. On the other hand, I know if I understood their language well, I would be less sensitive to the sound of it. But when they speak, it always seems to me as if they're yelling. Particularly so because when addressing us, they shout louder to make themselves better understood.

A soldier is sprawling on the grass in front of Madame Rose's house, a few meters from us. He's in the sun doing his total-nudism cure; even in wartime he's pursuing his nudist dream, his nudist meditations. Lying on his back, he is exposing himself completely. Madame Rose calls him a son of a bitch, disgusting. He doesn't understand the words, but he understands the intent.

We'll see him again, in regulation dress, accompanied by a *Feldwebel*, who speaks French and practices finesse.

"It is better," he tells us, "that you not understand what he told me . . ."

But he doesn't hesitate to give us a faithful summary of their conversation.

"Morality is lower in France than in Germany . . ."

He leans to one side and drops his hand toward the ground to better demonstrate the low level of morality in France.

At first I think he simply wants to humiliate us with this overview of two systems of morality, Eastern and Western. In fact, it's more nuanced. He alludes to the nude women in our magazines and, above all, to the lewd photography, some of which is excellent.

I'd be tempted to agree with him, bearing in mind that he has not indicted a morality but only a few examples of veiled pornography legal in France and banned in Germany. No doubt he's implying that Germany is virtuous and France dissolute, but I pay no mind.

Still, it's true that if Frenchmen were sensitive about the squalid or the frankly ugly, magazines of pornographic "artistry" would have no readers. Laws against pornography would be unnecessary. Which leads to contemplating the war and politics generally. In an ideal civilization, politics would concern only hygiene. And war would seem absurd. As much so as resolving a discussion about biology or a dispute about poetry with the use of force.

Meanwhile, in the courtyard another soldier, also dressed only in shorts, is playing hoops with a bicycle wheel and a tire pump. He is certainly older than thirty.

He's as serious as a judge. He's not excusing himself with a smile. He's playing alone, with a ferocious gravity.

While we're having lunch, the hoops player stretches out in a folding chair that had been left in front of the door. He's whistling, full-throatedly, nonstop, for a long time. He's giving himself a concert. He's whistling. He's not embarrassed.

Are they "badly brought up" or insolent?

They liberally distribute French hardtack (to animals) and cans of monkey meat. Their cars are full of it. They also distribute Algerian tobacco and packs of Gauloises bleues. They smoke only cigars and their straw cigarettes. It must be said that they offer these leftovers of requisitioning, or ransacking, simply, without arrogance or ostentation.

We'd finished dinner. Madame Rose lit an oil lamp from 1900 that has a black onyx base (the power lines had been cut). A soldier enters. We know him: we've often run into him at the well; he gave chocolate to Madame Rose's three-year-old nephew. He sits in the only wicker chair. This one is not dressed in shorts. He's wearing pants with suspenders—and no shirt. He settles into the chair and starts whistling, without worrying about us. I'm beginning to think that the art of whistling is peculiar to Germany. He's whistling: it's hard not to imagine some deliberate insolence. But no . . . He confides to us the reason he whistles. It's because he's always in a good mood: "*Ich bin immer lustig . . .*"

He asks Madame Rose's permission to use her table to write a letter.

"*Meine liebe kleine . . .*"

"Hurry up and go back to her already!" Madame Rose shouts at him. But he doesn't understand a word of French.

He writes with care, filling every inch of the page. When he's finished, he remains seated at the table. He seems to feel as if he's among family. And I swear that at that moment there's nothing that could be called malicious about the man. But he stays. We have to gesture to him that we're going to bed. I never saw one of those Germans who thought he was "de trop" anywhere.

The next day, he travels to Paris by truck. He returns in the evening stuffed with revealed truths: "The peace will be signed in a week to ten days . . . London is nearly destroyed . . ." I wonder whether he senses that such news isn't completely agreeable to us . . . I don't think so. I should add that at this point, the beginning of July, I had not met a French citizen other than those women in Les Douciers who accepted with pleasure the idea of a peace dictated unilaterally by Hitler. We had no news other than through a few German newspapers given us by the soldiers and editions of *Le Matin* and *Paris-soir* brought from Ladon that by all indications were written by the *Kommandantur*. (I'll say nothing of the news that sprang from thin air.) That's how it was announced to us, even before the armistice, that the constitution of 1875 had been abrogated and replaced by a dictatorship. False news can have a premonitory quality, at least as much so as dreams.

News given us by German soldiers is amazingly consistent. And not only the news but the commentary and opinions of the soldiers. Doubt doesn't seem to be a German virtue. It's true that if a German had doubts, he would keep quiet. It is said that news is transformed according to those who peddle it. That's not true for these German infantrymen. What they had been told in briefings, what they read in their newspapers and hear on their radios is repeated identically, without alteration, like a daily catechism, like a movement in a military drill. We never know their intent. Do they want to humiliate us? Do they want us to join in their joy as victors? Or to dissolve ourselves with them in some dream of a Pax Germanica? Do they want us to celebrate the end of the war with them? They are the victors and about to return home. At least they no longer risk being killed. Maybe they can't imagine that their joy isn't ours. A happy man can't stand the sadness of others, he nullifies it, to him his joy seems to project onto the universe.

One of them approaches us on the road to ask where he can find some chocolate. The vans of his field kitchens are full of chocolate. Maybe he's trying to get on the good side of a cook! As for finding chocolate at the grocer's in Chapelon or Ladon, he shouldn't count on it. He's a good-natured, brown-haired little fellow with a gentle manner, a bit dazed, a rare type among these soldiers. In wartime, it seems he's pursuing a dream of chocolate.

He shows us a pocket map, and on this map are the regions occupied by German troops and by the Italians. The line he traced with his finger was nearly accurate. But we didn't know that yet, and we thought his commanders were wrong.

They had all fallen for the same dogma. They all say war is abhorrent and Germany is innocent of it.

"Orléans, *kaput* . . . ," but German mortars are so intelligent that the cathedral wasn't hit, nor the statue of the *Jungfrau.**

"The war . . . bad thing for you, for us, for everyone . . .

"France, Belgium, Holland and Denmark were all under the influence of England . . . It is England that dragged these nations into making war on Germany . . . The proof is in war plans found in Bel-

* The Virgin.

gium . . . But it will take no more than two or three weeks to finish off England."

I remember we showed the soldier in search of chocolate the size of Denmark compared to Germany. This didn't shake him at all. I've rarely understood so clearly that not all men acquire certainty by the same means.

Abel Delaveau tries to explain to a few soldiers what he understands about the peace and the war. In substance, he says, "Daladier, Chamberlain, Göring, Hitler, all bastards . . ." Whatever effort he made to speak a pidgin, the soldiers didn't understand, and perhaps that was for the best. But his tone is one of such absolute conviction that the soldiers agree, nodding their heads.

A calf is lowing in the meadow behind the farmhouse. The Germans had taken it from who knows where, hoisted it into a truck and tethered it there. Abel thinks it's one of his calves; he jumps into the truck and is about to cut the tether with his knife . . . The Germans shout threats; in a word, they're yelling. A noncommissioned officer intervenes and is yelling too. Abel responds in the same tone of voice. The officer goes away for a moment then returns armed with his revolver, showing it to Abel. But Abel had been mistaken. It wasn't one of his calves. The officer had not leveled the gun at Abel's face. The revolver was only a symbol of the law of war. It all ended in laughter.

I have told it accurately, but this story about the calf only proves that Abel is not easily intimidated and that German soldiers don't systematically kill all civilians. The detail of a revolver shown but not aimed is individual. Another noncom might have put it more brutally. And what would have happened had Abel not been mistaken, if the calf had been one of his? It all varies according to the commander. The first soldiers who came through demanded wine at gunpoint. Their commanding officer, Abel told me, was "a real brute."

I haven't talked about Choum, the Siamese cat. I love animals, but I dislike a certain way of loving animals. I have a horror of people who bestow all the resources of their tenderness on a dog or cat. And I like it even less when literature joins in (like moths on a garment, as they say).

Nevertheless, I'll mention that we were reunited with Choum.

He tolerated the first days of the exodus well. The night we fled Chapelon, we had left him in the car. The door was open; he escaped. That was seventeen days ago. We find him on top of a pile of firewood. He meowed but did not approach. For seventeen days he'd had to live on scraps of meat thrown out by the Germans.

Finally, he lets himself be picked up. We bring him into our bedroom. He isn't afraid. But I can't say he seems deeply satisfied. He sits on my knees, jumps on the bed, looks for a nice spot, gives up, jumps on my lap again. This is still only the return from wildness to domesticity.

But that night he absolutely refused to sleep on a chair. He settles on the bed, up against me. (Never had I allowed nor sought such promiscuity.) That's when he sings the hymn of a cat reunited with man. It wasn't purring, much less meowing, it was a kind of whimper of joy, strange, high-pitched, that I had never heard from a cat, that continued till dawn and that he never did again.

As the sun sets, we're sitting on the bench against the front of the farmhouse. Some soldiers are wandering in the courtyard. An officer comes toward us and from a distance asks whose farm this is, who's the one in charge here. There are many ways to answer such a question. Abel leapt up. I had the impression he was charging the officer; he stopped right in front of him.

"I am . . ."

He says these words with his head and body projected forward and his hand against his chest, fingers spread like a claw.

He could not have expressed himself more clearly had he said, "I'm the master here; I tolerate you but I'm not afraid of you."

I thought of a tall devil with a face like Don Quixote who at the beginning of the 1914 war was at a crossroads in Woëvre at night sitting on his horse in a mess of jumbled-up regiments screaming, "Who's in command here?"

I wouldn't have the foolishness to say the German officer was afraid. But either he was troubled by such defiance or he gave up mystified; he walked away without a word.

I thought of you, Monsieur von Mützenbecher. Would a German peasant have made a stand like that?

Abel had told me about a conversation he'd had with a German noncommissioned officer, a twenty-year-old student, a day or two before our return to Chapelon. "All nations," Abel told him, "are responsible for the war. But Hitler is war itself." The young man started only when Abel said Hitler's name. And Abel, who distrusts smooth-talkers but appreciates eloquence, said to him, "You can't do anything to me. I prefer to die standing than live on my knees . . ."

But to me Abel says more simply, "They're here. We must endure them but not demean ourselves."

He tells me of a demeaning gesture. In Lorris, about thirty women were lining up in front of a bakery. They weren't used to that yet. They were jostling one another and soon were insulting each other. One of the women called out to a German soldier and asked him to "bring some order to all this." This German didn't love order as much as some others, or maybe he hadn't been given that assignment. He laughed.

Young anarchists before 1914 used to say quite readily, "What does it matter to us if the Germans invade Paris? . . . The trains will run better." But they weren't thinking that the inventiveness of a people, say, the Germans, might attack problems other than the railways while on foreign soil. But there isn't the same baseness in that as in accepting order at any price, such as their setting up "engineers of the soul."* In those distant times, among those Frenchmen who didn't align with the cardinal points of the political map, some had modesty in their nationalism, thought it indecent for a son to shout from the rooftops that he loves his mother. Others loved France as some of the insane love. Their love is a delirium of rage and jealousy, fed by base motives. They accuse their wives of vile or incestuous affairs.

While lost in these mediocre reflections I followed the sinuous curves of an old sideboard. My pipe and that old sideboard became my opium. But I don't want to lose hold of myself or my hold on what I call civilization. I'm not a man on a desert island; in any case

---

* A reference to writers, coined in 1932 by Stalin when he ordered them to tailor their themes to serve the state.

there are no more desert islands. Montaigne, Pascal, humanism. But watch out for pedants who trade in it, watch out for the petty shop-keepers of humanism.

If we are to believe the incoherent Radio France, France will have three governments: the *Kommandantur* in Paris, a government in Clermont-Ferrand and another in London. Plus that woman in Lor-ris and all those like her. This is the bottom. We've hit bottom. It's time to reinvent patriotism, to redefine nationalism. An opportune moment: people certainly no longer have any.

The field kitchen is set up under the shed next to Madame Rose's house. Two detachments have come for food, the first in gray-green and boots, the second in shorts . . . Floating comically above this undulation of bare shoulders are a few heads shaped like necks, such as the painter Grosz drew after the 1914 war, and the pointed head of a little *Herr Doktor* with eyeglasses.

An order. The detachment of men in shorts marches away in groups of four. But the man in front kicks his legs forward, goose-stepping, as a joke. I do my best to shake off a stupid idea: This sol-dier, however he can, is relieving oppression. He's mocking an entire regime. His leg kicked forward makes a dent in the regime. He's kicking Hitler.

One of the men from the field kitchen has grabbed a dress and apron that Madame Rose had washed and that were drying on the line. He's using them to scrub and polish the wheels. Madame Rose notices, snatches them from his hands and heaps insults on him: "You're 'bout to *see* out if I's washed this dress to clean your dirty grease." (In Chapelon they speak like this, and after my stay in Les Douciers, I like this way of speaking and it touches me, much more so than had I been born in the Gâtinais.) The field-kitchen men yell, "*Kaput!*" But they give in.

They polish the spokes vigorously with a brush. An hour later an officer inspects the field kitchen. It's like this in every army in the world, but with nuances. A French officer would no doubt have found that the spokes of the wheel were guilty of not shining like the rays of the sun. But the German officer makes a speech that could be heard from a distance. I call it a speech, for I can't manage to figure out whether he's scolding, reprimanding and threatening, or he's giving them a course in the technique of cleaning field-kitchen wheels. The tone is at once authoritarian and litanic. You'd think a prophet had come or that a preacher is preaching about the wheels of field kitchens.

A soldier is washing at the well. An athlete lifting weights is tattooed on his arm. Not a swastika or a portrait of Hitler. It's an athlete with bulging biceps. So the art of tattooing develops independently of regimes, faithful to itself.

I accompany Abel Delaveau into town. Ladon has about a thousand inhabitants. For days I've seen only a farmyard and, between the farm and Madame Rose's house, a haystack and a pile of beet pulp. Ladon seems like a big city to me.

Abel's brother-in-law, a retired schoolteacher, lives in Ladon. He had fled by bicycle with his wife. When he returned, his door had been broken down and was ruined, but he recovered his furniture.

It is indeed true that the Germans shot thirteen French soldiers and eight civilians. In Ladon, as in other French towns, there were attempts at resistance. A few civilians (refugees) had joined forces with soldiers. The Germans found them in a cellar, where two people from the town, an old man and his wife, were also hiding. The old couple, knowing the area well, was able to escape through the countryside. The Germans took the others and put them up against the wall. Traces of blood can still be seen. Then they threw incendiary grenades into the whole group of houses. Only sections of wall, debris, pitted facades and rubble remain.

The Germans dug two graves, one for the soldiers and one for the civilians . . . They planted two crosses. On one: *Dreizehn Soldaten*. On the other: *Acht Franzosen*. On each of the communal graves they threw some flowers.

"Do you know," a Monsieur D. tells us, "who is really responsible for France's defeat? The schoolteachers." I heard that this very morning. "Responsible because of what they taught and because, since they are practically all officers, they gave the signal that it was every man for himself."

I thought he was repeating the words of a madman or that this was the sign of some political delirium searching no matter where for personifications and symbols. But I've since heard the accusation again. And I recall the mystical pharmacist who declared with satisfaction that the war would at least have the excellent result that schoolteachers and members of parliament could no longer be paid.

"I've never made patriotism my business," Monsieur D. says with patriarchal solemnity, "but I fought in the other war, and I told my son, 'Do your duty . . .'"

His son is an officer trainee at Saumur and told him during a leave that all his schoolmates were fascists. That debate is outside my subject. I'm recounting and resisting commentary. But I notice that this war has exacerbated political hatreds and that partisans of order at any price, similar in this to revolutionaries hypnotized by the Russians, can't conceive of that order except with a foreign face. And I believe that France is Abel Delaveau and the old schoolteacher.

The charm of Ladon is a little river without embankments that runs between houses, framed by facades and foliage: an intimate river. It is a pleasant, quaint setting where the water seems ancient.

Some German soldiers got hold of a rowboat, probably the only one the river had ever known. The boat is gliding along, and one of the soldiers, standing in the bow, is playing the accordion.

They are only soldiers enjoying themselves. But they're acting serious. I'd swear they think they're charming us. They're gondoliers of victory, showing the vanquished how to use the right setting and the poetry of an accordion in a rowboat. I couldn't say why . . . but at that moment I recalled a strange restaurant in Berlin where I'd eaten a dozen years earlier. It was in an immense building. Each floor evoked a region, a province. Trompe l'oeil landscapes covered the walls. The waitresses were dressed ridiculously, some as Bavarians, some as Austrians. Everything was folkloric, comic opera and panorama.

The racket fills the silence enclosed by these facades, these falling leaves and this little stream. The accordion can be heard throughout the town. A hundred meters away a sentry stands guard in front of the town hall. A hundred meters away are the communal graves.

About thirty French prisoners are crammed into a garage in Chapelon. I'd like to chat with them, to learn about their war from them. It's difficult. They'll only say that they have no complaints about the Germans. Anything to tell? For them it all can be summarized like this: they were holding, they weren't discouraged, then suddenly it seemed as if they'd been freed from military discipline and turned loose on the roads, the way one frees a bird who doesn't know how to fly outside its cage. They weren't even given some routine explanation. Their silence contrasts with the talkative Germans. Stranger and more unexpected is that the Germans reveal more of themselves with isolated German words, which we can often make sense of only through their facial expressions.

A soldier is hanging his shirt on a clothesline in the sun. He's clumsy, he doesn't even know how to use the clothespins that are on the line. Madame Rose shows him how to do it. That's all. She doesn't say a word. Does she want to win the goodwill of the conquerors? No . . . she can't tolerate work badly done, she can't help herself. But these little favors, the canned monkey and tobacco handed out, even the gesture of making the shed, which the farm uses as a little workshop, off-limits to the troops, who had already stolen some tools, all create contact, a familiarity. History is difficult. France is large. Chapelon is small. A courtyard in Chapelon is smaller still. In principle the *Kommandantur*, since the departure of the "real brute," reprimands pilfering. Thus it's understandable that poor people might lose the right balance between submission under pressure and their sense of dignity.

This war isn't evolving like others. Hate hasn't been generated through the stereotypical images. It is quite remarkable that the word *Boches* is rarely heard anymore, and that the Germans have become "the Germans." But no less surprising to me is that the women don't say "the Germans" but rather "the soldiers," as if there were a kind of equivalence among all armies.

•

The Germans have left. We're hoping no more will come. Obviously, with a few months' hindsight, it was an absurd hope. But the word *occupation* did not have a well-defined meaning for us. The Germans are going back up to Paris and are going to return home. Chapelon is four kilometers from the main highway. Perhaps they'll forget about us.

They're gone. It's like peacetime. There's silence at dusk, as in all villages in peacetime. I say to Abel Delaveau, "The village resembles its old self."

"Yes . . . but not completely. The squeak of a horse cart or a bicyclist returning home is missing . . ."

The following day, new convoys go by on the road. The trucks follow each other at distances so absolutely equal that one thinks of a geometrical parade. The rumbling is continuous, a noise like gravel on a conveyor belt. Once again I feel as if everything that passes by on the road passes over me, that everything it bears, I bear.

Some officers get out of their cars and exchange very tense salutes. They train their binoculars on the rear of the convoy and on the sky, at three high-flying aircraft.

British aircraft, perhaps. Who said that? . . . I don't recall. It's our supreme hope and so seems like a wish for a miracle.

Meanwhile, in Ladon there's a rumor that Russia took Bessarabia, Poland and eastern Prussia. The Germans station a few cannons in a field under some trees. We conclude that they're being hidden from aircraft; we think the officers look worried.

The cannons remain in the field. An artillery unit installs itself in the village.

The cannons are in the orchard and soldiers in shorts are everywhere. We're under the domination of cannons and shorts. Oppression is cannons and shorts.

It's an artillery regiment of Saxons. They all insist on letting us know they're Saxons, but never fail to add that Saxons or Prussians, they're all Germans. In fact they're not as arrogant or sarcastic as the soldiers who were billeted in Les Douciers before the signing of the armistice. Nor are they completely like the soldiers who occupied Chapelon before that. But is it a difference of province or branch of the army? The others were infantrymen, these are artillerymen.

Indeed, they seem less absolutely military. They don't arrive at the field kitchens for food in tight ranks. They're capable of bringing their mess tins without obeying an order and without forming up in groups of four.

Although they're Saxons, they are no less capable of astonishing military perfection when they assemble for roll call in the farm courtyard. They are perfectly straight, still and uniform when standing at attention. Their eyes-right and eyes-left are masterpieces of interchangeable mechanics. Even their enthusiasm is military. As much as left-face and eyes-left, the guttural orders and responses are prescribed by theory. At each command they all shout, "*Heil!*" (I believe!). One might think of the shouts of admiration or howls of laughter heard not long ago in mess halls or those "artistic" basement cabarets. But more forceful. More like the brutal, imperative honk of a car horn. I don't understand what the officer is saying to them. He's chanting, raucously, but chanting.

The field kitchen is no longer under the shed next to Madame Rose's house. It is directly in front of Abel Delaveau's door. They put it there to be near the well, no doubt. It is impossible to enter the house without passing the cooks, their friends or groups of soldiers getting food. That doesn't bother them.

I go into the house from time to time to avoid seeing them, to forget them. Then I feel an instant relief, as if I were getting into a bath after a long walk. We ache from Germans.

They're clean. They wash at the well, torsos bare. They plunge their heads into the bucket. But it's not exactly what we call cleanliness. It's an exhibition of cleanliness. They could put you off water forever. Civilization isn't solely a pump, a tap or even a shower. I'd already felt this in the Far East when I saw the Europeans, so proud of their hydrotherapy facilities.

They're cheerful, but what laughter! A laughter that comes from the perineum and that the throat amplifies like a loudspeaker. Will we ever dare laugh again?

They want to be courteous. But if they want to speak to you and you turn your back on them, they never hesitate to touch your shoulder.

The cook announces that Spain has taken Gibraltar. This is surely from *Völkischer Beobachter*.* All news they find agreeable they assume is agreeable to everyone.

Day and night a sentry, weapon slung over his shoulder, goes round the village. At night he passes right near our window. The noise of his boots drowns out the sound of the horses bumping against their stalls and the magic flute of the toads.

They march by fours wearing bathing suits, in step, singing. But their song is militarized, determined by the soldiers' manual and orderly as a drumroll. They sing sometimes every fourth step, sometimes every eighth step. Sometimes the song gets louder and sometimes their footfalls mark time. This mixture of nudism on parade and singing brings to mind a Surrealist joke or those cartoons of a nude Negro in a top hat.

They may be ridiculous. But as the peasants say, they're the masters. On a wall in front of the town hall the *Kommandantur* has put up an official notice in German and French. The French translation is dubious but not obscure: "To the occupied populations . . . Occupation troops must treat the populace with care, provided it remains peaceful." No one had promised to treat me with care yet. "It is prohibited to listen to non-German radio stations in public or in groups, with the exception of a foreign radio station authorized by headquarters."

A rumor circulates that an order has been given to bring all radios to the town hall. The rumor was never confirmed.

"On the wireless," Madame Rose reports, "they said that male refugees must get back on foot, that women and children would be brought home."

They're saying . . . Now we depend on what "they're saying."

"Based on whether one is headstrong or not," Madame Rose says, "one could very well go to prison . . ."

He's colossal, a colossus perforated by two blue eyes. Who knows why his eyes are in the middle of his face. They could be anywhere else on his body without it being a surprise. The contours of his face

* The Nazi party newspaper.

are in fact hardly more delicate than the contours of a thigh or fore-arm. This colossus is sitting on the bench next to me. And he's telling me his life story. He is thirty-one. He enlisted for twelve years and has already done eight. His three brothers are soldiers as well. He's a corporal, a longtime corporal. He is proud of his rank and his se-niority in that rank. The day he was promoted to corporal was a big day . . . He went through Romorantin and Orléans; he did his duty, he served his country (*Plficht . . . Vaterland**) and was lucky enough not to be wounded and to have kept his good health.

He also talks to me about the occupation of the Rhineland by the French and England, which is responsible for the war. But very little, less than the others. International politics is not his forte. He men-tions it only out of consideration, in case I'm not in possession of the truth he gets from briefings, the way he gets his rations from the field kitchen. He's sharing with me.

The next day I pretend not to recognize the colossal corporal. But in vain. He comes straight for me and brings me three packs of ciga-rettes . . . Two days later, I flee again. But he has other confidences in store for me. Pointing to his officer, he tells me the man is only twenty-one and has no experience. He tells me a rather long story, which I understand very poorly. I think it's about a scrape, when the experienced corporal had to make up for the shortcomings of the young officer, whose knowledge comes only from schools.

Everything I will try in order to escape the colossal corporal will be in vain. He brings me packets of tobacco, packs of cigarettes. It's only looted tobacco. But then he brings me a box of cigarettes that had been sent him by his "mamma." And ten times he repeats ten-derly, "Mamma . . . Mamma! . . ."

I have no doubts: the colossal corporal needs a confidant. He's not finding any in his army. And it's me he has chosen, for reasons only God knows. He's looking for human intimacy. He is thick-skinned. No matter; I understand that in his fashion he's looking for what Montaigne calls, "the exercise of souls, with no other fruit."

I have to tell everything about the colossal corporal, we'll see

---

* Duty . . . fatherland.

why later on. We'll see what contrasts a man can show, even a reen-
listed corporal, even a German. The colossal corporal approached
the bench where we were sitting. One of Abel Delaveau's neighbors,
wounded in the last war, was showing me his atrophied arm and
unusable hand, which he almost always kept gloved. But he had removed the glove. The hand was white and thin, with pink fingernails,
pathetically like that of a woman of leisure, while the other was a
peasant's hand, large and calloused. The farmer rolled up his sleeve:
the arm was skeletal. Then the corporal, offering a comparison, smiling wide, also rolled up his sleeves, and crossing his arms made his
athletic biceps bulge.

I thought: That's Germany. And for a long time I could not resist
this too-simplistic idea.

We're being "kept." Soldiers are handing out cans of monkey, sardines and "*zalmon*," chocolates and candy. But they are all French
brands. Everything comes from Rouen or Orléans; everything had
been looted. When we were sitting on the grass with the Aufresnes
a few kilometers from Les Douciers, a German soldier handed us a
can of monkey. That was the first time. And we were hungry and had
nothing else to eat. Had I been alone I might have refused this gift
from the conqueror.

I say *might have*. In these things one shouldn't commit lightly.
One shouldn't judge categorically or translate honor into a written
code. It's all circumstance; everything depends on nothing, on a look.
That day, I didn't have to decide for myself. I wasn't the one taking the
canned monkey from the soldier's hand. But I ate some like everyone else.

This becomes a game. Everyone shows off the soldiers' gifts the
way they would show off booty. Rustics don't have a casuistry for
points of honor. After all, it's not submission, it's more repossession.
Anyway, we're prisoners of a sort, and prisoners don't uphold honor
by letting themselves die of hunger.

The field kitchen, as I've said, is in front of the farmhouse kitchen.

The bench is a good observation post. The colossal corporal is emptying a bottle of wine in a single draft, without taking his lips from the mouth of the bottle. He's filling himself with wine the way he would fill a fuel tank. A soldier has a chocolate bar in one hand and a slab of butter in the other. Alternately, he bites into the chocolate and the butter.

The soldiers have stolen some eggs and some potatoes. The potato stealers must not be rurals. They've pulled up the foliage without digging deeper and have unearthed only some tubers the size of three pinheads.

They threw an artillery cartridge in Abel Delaveau's pond. The fish are floating belly-up. Sometimes you complain, sometimes not. The *Kommandantur* is all-powerful. Nobody knows whether it's better to endure or to protest.

Some beehives had been set up next to an old windmill. Its sails had long ago been detached and the old wooden beams piled next to the beehives. Some soldiers had set fire to the hives and the beams. Presumably these honey thieves were just clumsy, but why had they set fire to the windmill blades?

I went over to the windmill. The sails were still burning. A swarm was buzzing around, stranded in front of a half-charred hive.

If I'm far from the farm for long I feel doubly exiled. I can't manage to put together this sky and those clumps of trees. The crops are so closely spaced that the countryside looks like a department store with innumerable counters of wheat and oats.

A German soldier asks to buy some milk. He's in bathing trunks. But he is polite. He salutes with a quick nod and a bow. His costume and the bow are incongruous, it seems to me. But do the Germans have a sense of the ridiculous? And he had doubtless forgotten that he was in a bathing suit.

These Saxon artillerymen are not the same Germanic type as the infantrymen who occupied the village before them. We're no longer seeing death's heads topped with flax. Most of these are brown-haired, very southern types. But brown-haired or blond, their ideas come from the same factory. Their field kitchen of news is a perfect machine. No doubt their newspapers are identical, but they digest them identically. Hitler loves peace and only England wanted war.

They are intrusive. But does the word have any meaning for them? They all ask what my profession is. I didn't understand the word *Beruf*. By analogies and gestures they revealed its meaning to me. It was so difficult that I momentarily forgot about the war and responded like an interrogated schoolboy. I was no longer in an occupied country but in fourth grade, reviewing columns of words in an old glossary.

A soldier washing his clothes in a bucket raises his head and says to us, "England is at war with France." This news seems grossly absurd to us. It goes without saying that we can imagine nothing of the real facts that it distorts and translates into propaganda.

He offers us a copy of *Völkischer Beobachter*. An entire page is filled with death announcements, each framed by a black line . . . Each concerns a soldier dead at the front, not only for Germany but "*Für Führer und Vaterland.*"

The cooks are peeling vegetables. On a chair they have set up a phonograph, which is spewing waltzes. The soldiers shout and bawl, raking up big shovelfuls of verbal rubble. The courtyard's peace is violated. We're no longer even masters of our own silence.

The noncommissioned officers eat their meals inside the farmhouse living room, kitchen and dining room. Abel Delaveau is no longer master, after God, of his own table. But for the moment there is no force that could chase them from that house. They pay no attention to us, and we pretend to ignore them.

But it's not the same with the cooks. They use the oven for the "gourmet meals." With words and gestures Madame Delaveau demanded they use their own coal and not any of hers. They gave in. They offered a little coffee, a little salt.

One evening we were all sitting on the bench in front of the house. They brought their phonograph. It's not a concert just for them. It's a concert for us. They're offering us a waltz by Johann Strauss, a crass female music-hall singer and a comic of the Ouvrard genre.* We form two groups with no hostility but with no connection.

One of the cooks has brought a German grammar. He is sitting next to Madame Rose's sixteen-year-old daughter. They're looking at a vocabulary exercise together. It was straightforward, with nothing questionable. The young girl doesn't pose a problem. She's not a peasant girl; she works at a monotonous job as a seamstress, dreaming, no doubt, of Paris and its big department stores. These Saxon and Rhenish soldiers are nothing to her but young people on vacation.

It's a spectacle that would have been intolerable for revanchists, Fourteenth of July parade-goers and music-hall patriots. But those types have disappeared, and they aren't missed. Even so, I ask myself whether in all wars there aren't these contacts between conquered populations and victorious soldiers. Historians and novelists neglect them, because they want their texts to be edifying and discreet, because such unfortunate details break with the party line, spoil their crude imagery.

Though Abel says to me, "Individually, they are men, like us," he feels the way I do, that any submission beyond what the enemy may force by coercion is always questionable. Madame Rose thinks more simply that past eight in the evening girls should not banter with soldiers, and she orders her daughter to bed.

We are eating, and eating well. We have rediscovered the ritual of mealtimes, momentarily forgotten. We are sleeping in a good bed. But we know nothing about our son and his two friends. Though I'm repeating to my wife that "nothing can have happened to them," I end up imagining the worst. I see them lying in a ditch, dying of hunger or wounded. I see my errant son searching for a morsel of bread. Did they return to Paris? Are they in Tournus, Trévoux, Saint-Amour, three possible destinations where they'd be safe? No way to

* Father-and-son singer-songwriters Éloi (1855–1938) and Gaston (1890–1981) Ouvrard popularized comic songs about military life.

communicate with them. And we are stuck, as they may be. Even if we had gasoline, where would we look for them? It's always the same empty deliberation in a vacuum.

We're leading a strange life that is attached to nothing apart from the kindness and sensitivity of the Delaveaus. We're prisoners, isolated from everything. We're receiving only information about the repairing of power lines and the reestablishment of train and mail service. The most tragic, most contradictory rumors circulate about political and military events. Convincing or crazy, they are distorted from mouth to mouth. Seemingly born by spontaneous generation, they transform politics into clichés, they're nothing but the fabrications of fear, they stave off a hunger for certainty that nothing can feed. Machine-gun fire is less depressing.

It is said that at the Gien and Sully bridges the Germans threw cars, bicycles and baby carriages into the water to clear the roadway faster. The story has a surprising precision: at the Gien bridge, the German guarding the left-hand sidewalk removed the babies before throwing their carriages into the Loire, but the German guarding the right threw everything, babies and carriages, into the water.

Today, July 4th, a soldier shows us a German newspaper from June 29th: Paul Reynaud's car overturned on the Saint-Tropez road. Marshal Balbo died in aerial combat. He was "a great friend of Germany."

The smallest gift of what we call civilization is that the details of events, if not their meaning, don't escape us. But this hamlet in the Gâtinais is as far from events as the Sahara. And never were the fates of individuals as closely tied to what we call history as during this war. Our life consists of waiting, anxiety and the passage of time.

The colossal corporal would very much like to chat with me, to tell me again in pidgin German the big events of his life, to show me the photograph of his wife again. Yesterday he told me what he counts on doing when he's out of the service. But I couldn't understand whether the profession he was describing with the gesture of two arms in the air and the words "*Schwarzer Mann*" was that of a miner, a coal maker or a chimney sweep. I flee. And yet I see that he's hiding two packages of tobacco in his hand. I've never shown such dignity. He is disconcerted. He salutes me formally. As he would a commanding officer. Everything is correct, a regulation salute, except the slightly disappointed smile he adds.

The best moment of the day is when Abel Delaveau brings back a cartful of forage. I help store it in the barn. Then we sit on the bench, or in the living room if it's empty of Germans, and we chat.

But mostly I ponder time, the passing of time. Counterrevolutionaries played the clavichord in Coblentz; revolutionaries before 1914 drank tea in London or Zurich, reconstructing the world in their imaginations. History allowed them their little corners, not us.

I've already said how I rewrote history. Now I set up a veritable workshop for historical repairs. History obeyed my commands. Victory breaks Germany as defeat would have.

I even invented an electromagnetic device. A recurring daydream. "Isn't my idea excellent, Saint-Exupéry?" In each airplane I placed a tube whose rays explode all motors not equipped with an equalizer tube.

I feel all the stupidity of the war weighing on me. Like between 1916 and 1918. But the other stupid war was fed by passions. Since the defeat, it seems to me the French masses contemplate events the way peasants watch hail falling. I've seen the face of defeat on soldiers fleeing along the roads; I have not seen it on civilians. And I had lived through only the defeat, not yet those days to come when it seemed as if a people were surrendering itself. But weren't you an internationalist? (An idiot . . . as Abel Delaveau and thousands of peasants would put it.) Yes, but not since the concept lost its meaning. One can't unite nothing with nothing. And the resignation itself was repugnant. If I had seen some other nation suddenly consent to French domination because France had been victorious, I'd have despised that nation.

There's bliss among the German soldiers, an expansion of self. A single idea in each head, but an idea without roots, an interchangeable idea revealed each day. Each day they're ready for a new revelation.

Walled in; we're walled in. In the village, there's someone who really is walled in. I could go share his prison. He is the longtime priest of Chapelon who, after thirty years' ministry, was banned. The woman who was the cause of his ban lives with him. She can be seen around the village, but he never crosses the threshold of his walled garden. Such is Abel Delaveau's natural nobility that in his account of this priest's story there is not a single coarse detail to be found, no food for scandal. And yet God knows how little Abel loves religion.

I'm becoming apathetic. Chapelon is a kind of ivory tower, or simply a burrow. My boundaries are the cannons under the orchard trees, the field kitchen in the courtyard, the haystacks and the roofs. But I can no longer look at the lines of trucks passing along the road. I close my eyes. I try not to hear. I'd like to stay like that, waiting for history to let me live.

At the door of the town hall–schoolhouse, a German officer politely makes way for my wife. He hesitates, then suddenly says in passable French, "You are afraid of us, madame?"

"Afraid? No, monsieur. But as long as you wear that suit (she points at his uniform) here, you are my enemy."

"But our Führer did not want war. It is France that declared war."

"I've read *Mein Kampf* . . ."

The officer seems embarrassed and responds, "We're changing . . . one can change, and the fault is England's, which, I swear in the name of Jesus, wants to dominate the world."

Such dialogue makes sense only through its tone and intent. The "you are afraid of us?," the "are we so terrible after all?" were clichés uttered by hundreds of Germans at the beginning of the occupation. This one blamed only the English. But most often total responsibility for the war was attributed to the English and the Jews, or even the Jews alone. Delirious interpretations, illusions personified, fabricated scapegoats. And Gutenberg's invention isn't free of blame: At the behest of the worst interests, it spreads the emptiest abstractions, devoid of bone and flesh. The Jews, instigators of carnage? Why not blame raccoons or the platypus?

"The 1875 constitution is abolished. Flandin is dictator." The farmhouse living room is lit by an oil lamp. (We have no electricity, the lines were cut.) Its light throws deep shadows on faces. A light from days gone by. Abel and I are sitting opposite each other. This news drops between us like a fly on the table.

We agree immediately that there is perhaps a dictatorship, but not this dictator. A dictator needs a little legend and a lot of popularity, enough at least so crowds join the police in cheering when he passes by.

The ones who most praise the wisdom of peasants are the same ones who deplore the passions of politics. They suggest that peasants are spared such passions, that they draw their wisdom straight from the soil. I've rarely seen a peasant who wasn't a "political animal." True, men of the soil have a politics of butter, just as workers have a politics of wages and bourgeois have, or had, a politics of annuities. But how crude that is. It's not true that ideas and feelings are never more than a transmutation, a sublimation of interests. At any rate, whenever I've chatted with peasants, I've always admired their political sense. They're not fooled by reversible ideas with which workers are sometimes exalted and other times bullied. And they resist those vast syntheses that semi-cultured bourgeoisie juggle.

Chapelon is in fact divided into two clans: the whites and the reds. The Montargis newspapers were teasing out of each commune the reasons for the polemic. A boy from Chapelon, playing with the carbine from a shooting gallery, wounded a little girl. The parents of one being from the "left" and the other from the "right," a Montargis newspaper made the accident into political vengeance.

An old man in the village, whose patriarchal courtesy I love—one of those old people who are likened to a gnarled tree stump (hackneyed but accurate)—tells me that a big jeweler from Paris had taken refuge in Chapelon. This retailer, who was traveling with gold ingots in his car, was rejoicing that the Paris police and the *gardes mobiles* were intact. This way Belleville and Billancourt would surely be kept in line. (I'd heard nearly the same words from Aufresne's mouth at Les Douciers.)

The old peasant invited him to keep quiet and told him such language wasn't appreciated in Chapelon.

This happened in the Gâtinais. But I know regions where the

workers are regarded as "profiteers," where their unrest is feared and there isn't the generosity to forgive them for having allowed fewer casualties during the 1914 war than the rural inhabitants.

I'm told that the B.'s are the area's rich people. They have numerous farms that they rent out, and in Chapelon they raise only two cows and some chickens. They are noted, without an excess of goodwill, to be in perpetual conversation with a German noncommissioned officer who wears an aviator's uniform. This is a very strange character who lurks almost everywhere and seems to attend roll call as if he were a guest. I believe, like everyone else, that he serves as a stool pigeon. Though I never had proof, B. is accused of . . . exchanging undignified words with the German and shamelessly comparing a France wholly devoted to fun with an orderly, hardworking Germany. A rumor is going round that he invited the aviator to dinner.

I think of the stories we were told about the 1870 war, about the silent and disdainful pride the enemy ran up against. True or not, these stories have the same significance. In either case they testify to how we wanted to appear.

When I was a small child, I heard the story of my aunt Léonie's handshake told a hundred times, a story that, as in all families, was polished and definitive, perfect as a work of art.

During the 1870 war one of my uncles, an engineering officer, had been taken prisoner in Sélestat. After the armistice, my aunt was allowed to go see her husband. Here I have only my childhood memories. They consist of a historical tableau: my uncle is shut up in a fortress, a bunker or perhaps a dungeon. A German officer leads my aunt to him down gloomy corridors, opens a door, salutes nobly and leaves.

The essence is that, for a few hours or a few days, the officer relaxed the regulations. He was so humane that it posed a problem for my aunt that for another woman would have been only elementary civility and decency. But she had an austere morality, left nothing to chance, and all her feelings, including her patriotism, were uncompromising. For her this was not a problem, it was a matter of conscience. Before returning to France, should she respond to the officer's salute by an inclination of the head? Or, to show her gratitude and not be outdone in nobility, should she offer him a handshake? My aunt thought the laws of war authorized extending her hand. She held out her hand. Oh, her body rigid and an indication, a hint, of a handshake! But after such deep deliberation! And it was one of the family's legends. Also, I believe that thirty years later my aunt still had qualms.

I was only beginning to perceive among some Frenchmen (Soutreux and Lerouchon were simply monsters) a disappearance of all national decency or a genuflecting to some supposed face of order, of absolute order, of order that discounts any human resistance. Or maybe they believe, as was once true and may be true again, that the war was not so much a combat between peoples as a settling of political scores. But how can we believe that this war is anything but the old diplomatic game or even an economic battle? I seem to be watching a part of France unite with Germany and murder Pascal.

It's Sunday. The French prisoners who are housed with farmers meet the colossal corporal at the inn. Everyone has his own liter, and the colossal corporal toasts with a vengeance. This does not scandalize me at all. It's something between combatants. It conforms with the rites of war as practiced before 1914. It even conforms with the infantry manual (it ought to be corrected), which says something like, outside combat, opposing armies should treat each other as comrades and give each other assistance.

Abel Delaveau asked for a prisoner. A farmer from near Dijon who fought at the Somme arrives glum and silent. Men of the soil aren't effusive. The first day he uttered a single phrase, "I know how to load a wagon." It was in front of the stable in response to a question Abel was asking him. He ate his meals with Abel. In two days he was transformed. From a zoo animal he turned back into a young peasant. But he didn't like to talk about the war, the defeat or his captivity. I saw many soldiers like that, avoiding the war the way some people don't like to talk about their illnesses.

Very different was a prisoner from the Vaucluse who was placed at a neighboring farm. He'd inspire terror, if his air of ferocity were to be believed. But it's only an air, a southerner's mimicry. He recounts clearly, in distinct tableaux, artfully, dramatically. Is he telling the truth? Modifying? Exaggerating? I have no idea.

"We were betrayed . . . sold out . . .

"There were seven of us left from the regiment; I'm saying the regiment, not the company . . .

"My commander escaped twice, and twice he was recaptured . . .

"The colonel blew his brains out. He said, 'The Germans won't get a word from me.'

"But the captain, in civilian life a big coal merchant, opened his bag in front of me and pulled out civilian clothing; he put it on . . . I said to him, 'Captain, only mountains never meet . . . we'll run into each other again.' He said, 'You'll be killed before that.' He joined his son; they took off together . . ."

German trucks are flying up the road at sixty-five kilometers per hour. In a field an old woman, her head wrapped in a kerchief, a *fanchon*, and an old man bent at the waist are digging for potatoes. I turn my back on the trucks. The village and the whole countryside are covered with Germans. At Madame Rose's the women are crocheting: "Reduce to sixteen." These magic words and the movement of the crochet hooks obsess me.

"They said . . ." The mysterious "they," the "they" of wars and revolutions; the "they" that means the powerful, the earth's great; the "they" that now means only the Germans.

They said some French ships had been sunk by the English. They said that there was a red army in France organized by Reynaud. With Abel Delaveau I try to make sense of the lies and absurdity, to detect in them a French wish or German intent. The news, the rumors allegorize vague political passions, they muddle the possible and the impossible, fabricate a monster out of distant associations (Reynaud raising a red army*).

But when I talk with Abel, I feel full of hope. I'm unaccustomed to such large events. I need a sharp mind. He has one, and that keenness

---

* Paul Reynaud (1878–1966), prime minister when Germany invaded, was a pro-business, center-right politician, but in the 1930s he endorsed military alliance with the Soviet Union.

is a gift. A strange illusion: when I chat with Abel it seems as if all the stupidity of the war is eliminated. It's as if I'd just won a victory.

Madame Rose brings us some news. This is proven, verified. A typist from Ladon, an educated woman, not one of those women who repeat nonsense, "heard it on the wireless."

"If Germany has not withdrawn its troops by the fourteenth, America comes in swinging . . ."

Today is July 10th. I too, after all, am losing myself in a dream of childish corrections of history.

Madame Delaveau surprises a soldier in the barn stealing an egg. He hides it awkwardly in his pocket . . . She calls him a thief and threatens him with the *Kommandantur*. Words spin round each other like billiard balls. The peasant woman expresses herself in a single stream, without punctuation. The German, angry, replies with shouts and gestures. She's speaking French; he's speaking German. They can't understand each other except by tone and gestures. The German gives in and returns the egg.

I know I'm not recounting a big event. But there are no small events. A person and his nation are wholly within the smallest act. Knowledgeable psychologists have said this in different language. I'm surprised the soldier gave in, not immediately like a shamed thief but after having shouted and threatened. I saw in that the effect of a decision from above, of an order from headquarters. Hitler's Germany, for the moment, does not want to rule solely by terror. A game is being played with the firing squad in Ladon, the prohibition on petty theft and their "Are we so terrible after all?" And the moderation the official notice advised for soldiers "if the population remains peaceful" is that much easier if they eat their fill, if they have all the stores they have requisitioned or looted since the defeat.

Behind this soldier is the entire might of the Reich, and the eyes of German soldiers are "full of victory," as a peasant said to me. I'm obsessed by the idea that between this soldier and myself there is no man-to-man relationship or any relation determined by the laws and customs of a common country. There's only the law of war, which is nothing but utility and caprice. Between him and me, it is understood that he has the power of life or death.

His belt buckle shines. On it I can read distinctly, "*Gott mit uns.*" The idea of God seemed obscure to me. There you have the dangers of popularization.

I was boss of the farm. Abel being out gathering forage, his wife asked me to stay with her and her two daughters. Seated on the bench, I'm guarding the farmhouse door. I'm protecting the women and children and reigning over twenty hectares of hay, beets and wheat. But I'm nothing more than the presence of a man. A silly man trying hard to give energy to his features and firmness to his gaze.

The following day, little Jacqueline comes looking for me. Near the outside of the courtyard wall, Madame Delaveau is talking with a group of soldiers. They surround one of those farm machines that look like an instrument of torture; it is a machine that pulls up weeds. She's afraid they want to take it.

"Ask them what they are doing . . ."

I manage to make my "*Warum*" and "*Was wollen Sie*"* understood. But I understand nothing of their responses. They all speak at once and yell to be better understood. Nonetheless, the German language is sometimes intelligible. The word "*reparieren*" saved everything. One of the soldiers is in fact straightening one of the cultivator's tines with a pair of pliers and an adjustable wrench. And I manage to gather that it had been hit by one of their trucks. But beforehand I had been very weak. The colossal corporal was passing by. He approached. I responded warmly to his "*Guten Tag.*" The others understood that we knew each other. I cravenly appeased the powerful.

I know I almost sound as if I'm joking and relating the infinitesimal. But we never knew which of these small incidents would be the last. And one would like to think that in each of these contacts with the German conquerors, small as it might be, something of our dignity is involved. I pity anyone who doesn't feel this. And if he is some kind of theorist in whom the presence of Germans arouses no sense of nationalism, I say I don't like the prisoner who flatters his jailer.

And the Germans are everywhere. Their life is superimposed

* Why . . . What do they want.

on that of the village, overloading it. They can no more be avoided than a line of ants on a garden path. Their private conversations that resemble barking, their raucous commands, the sound of a single soldier's boots, or a detachment marching in step, their singing in chorus, which is nothing but cadenced footfalls from their throats, drown out the countryside and drown out the village. Their trucks are still filing toward Paris, northward, each carrying on the front, atop the canvas roof, a figurehead, an ironic trophy: one of our gas masks.

Two young girls are said to have been raped by soldiers in the woods. It's more than unlikely this will ever be mentioned again.

Under a sky sometimes deep blue, sometimes gray from passing clouds, I'm walking with Abel Delaveau on the farm's little lane that runs perpendicular to the road. It's unbelievable that a truck would leave the road and turn onto this path. Yet one of their trucks turns sharply onto the cart path without slowing down. We didn't hear it. And the driver said nothing. He hit the brakes five meters from us and blew the horn. We only just had time to get out of the way. The driver is irate. For him there are no small lanes or country lanes or lanes reserved for horse carts or dreaming. There are only some universal rules of traffic.

In the evening, a few soldiers form a circle around Madame Rose's nephew. If this little boy wanted to describe Germans, he'd no doubt say Germans stole candy in order to bring him sweets. The soldiers point out with respect one of them who is a pastor and speaks French. If the pastor had been alone, who knows what he would have said to me. But our brief conversation was uninteresting. We agreed that Dresden is a beautiful city. (For that matter, I rarely heard the Germans talk about a city, even a foreign one, without adding that it's beautiful.) And he asked if the French read Goethe.

We return to our room. Not even the night is empty of Germans. The sentry and his boots pass in front of our window. But I love the sound, like bombing in the distance, of the farm horses bumping against their stalls.

This morning, the fake aviator, the stool pigeon, accosted me in the hallway that leads to the farmhouse bedrooms . . . He approaches everyone the same way: "Excuse me . . . I want to improve myself in the French language . . ."

He's a strapping lad, a good-looking boy, with regular but flabby features, a saccharine face. Because I've been told he speaks French very fluently, I have the feeling that his difficulty finding words and embarrassed pronunciation are nothing but a ruse. Doubtless he wants to dispel my idea that he has been in France as a spy for a long time. In a few seconds I'm certain he's no aviator but rather an informant or a gadfly. Above all, he's an imbecile. He's more of an imbecile than he is a German. He asks me questions about grammar and proper word usage. And doubtless to compensate me, he tells me about his stay in Paris, after the arrival of the Germans. "Paris is a beautiful city." The three essential stops of his visit were Fouquet's Restaurant, the Arc de Triomphe and Napoleon's tomb.

If he is a spy, he isn't the stealthy kind that glides along walls. He's clingy, frightfully clingy. He sticks.

Abel Delaveau drove us into Montargis in his Citroën. But he was wise enough to also bring along the German soldier who guards the prisoners at Chapelon. The most straightforward men often show an unexpected cleverness in the worst of circumstances, when the clever get lost in detail. The German walks into the *Kommandantur* as if he were at home. He obtains a coupon for ten liters of gasoline. We go to the tanker. There's no army, even the German army, whose disciplinary structure doesn't conceal cracks that resourcefulness can slip through. Whether the German is acting out of kindness or vanity, I don't know. We are given all the gasoline we can carry. We buy a watering can that we'll stopper however we're able, with bits of rag. Need I say that Abel shared this treasure with me? But I'm still thirty liters short of hoping to reach the Jura or the Saône-et-Loire.

Women line up at store doors. But there's no line for German soldiers. They go to the front. One shopkeeper, asked for I don't know what foodstuff, says angrily, "The Parisians looted it all." The Parisians, that's the horde of refugees. The sentry in front of the *Kommandantur* roughly pushes away passersby. I'm already drawing vast ethnic conclusions, but I'm suddenly reminded of that French sergeant on the road in a frightened, authoritarian frenzy, yelling, flinging cart horses around by their bridles and taking out his rage on the gearboxes of cars. The terrace of the café is occupied solely by German officers, stiff in their chairs, like gilded idols stuck to the sidewalk.

We find an edition of *Le Matin*. We read that "England coldly committed the greatest crime of all time," that she "proved her bestial cruelty and, in a few hours, beat all records for collective criminality and moral baseness."* We also read that General de Gaulle "has been discharged for his conduct." A local newspaper, *Le Gâtinais*, reprints the provisions of the armistice.

* On July 3, 1940, in the port at Mers-el-Kébir, Algeria, negotiations to guarantee that French ships would not fall into German hands failed, and British vessels fired on the French fleet, killing 1,297 Frenchmen.

V

THE COLOSSAL CORPORAL.
RETURN TO THE FREE ZONE

At dusk, the colossal corporal brings me a veritable parcel of cigarette packs. By words and gestures he invites me to bring it into the
house immediately. So this is more than accepting a gift, there's some
complicity. What's strangest is that the colossal corporal has noticed
my coldness. I don't know how he interprets it, but he accepts it. He
no longer hangs around us.

He came back the following day, in the evening, accompanied by
a comrade, a haircutter from Dresden who makes for an astonishing
contrast. He is small, brown-haired, with lively eyes. Later I thought
the colossal corporal had brought him to express by means of words
and his intelligence the mute sentiments the corporal himself felt, a
sort of ambassador from the realm of the soul. But this young soldier
doesn't speak a word of French, no more than the colossal corporal
does. And I know less than a hundred words in German. He speaks
at length. I understand that he hoped to return home soon, that a
peace treaty would soon be signed and we'd see no more of these
pointless wars: "*Ohne Zweck*."* But I don't know whether he means
that all war is pointless or that the Pax Germanica will henceforth
render all war useless. Especially since he is leaving us to go listen to
the latest news on the radio. He calls that news. I'd very much like to

* Without purpose.

tell him that's easy to say. I settle for asking whether the news seems interesting and truthful to him. He innocently responds yes.

From *Radio de Paris* we learn at least one true fact: Marshal Pétain is the head of state. It also announces to us that France is a courageous country but shockingly gullible; that its health relies on a return to the soil; that minds must change, not just the constitution; and that the snarled traffic on the roads, the muddling of refugees with the army in flight, was England's work. So Germany is in possession not only of France's soil but also its airwaves. This massive propaganda has no finesse. But, alas, Germany didn't create this linguistic game using flimsy prototypes.

I can easily tell that my wife is less and less able to endure her worry about our son. And each day I have more trouble disguising mine. This is when the miracle intervenes, the hand of God or man righting the course of things, the stagnation of the world. I was with Abel Delaveau in his garage. We were estimating the length of my route and the amount of gasoline necessary. That's when the colossal corporal's face appeared in the doorway. In shadow, his face was even more featureless. But his eyes, like one long blue line between the fatty rolls of his eyelids, were beseeching, imploring, like only the eyes of a faithful dog can be. His head was nearly touching the roof beams. He seemed like one of those giants who lift the globe.

Abel has a much better sense of the moment and of people than I do. And I still can't manage to grasp how, without knowing a word of their language, he almost always made the Germans understand. Don't say by gestures. Others also know how to gesticulate. By his expression, I think, and by I don't know what mesmerism. The corporal grasped perfectly that for lack of thirty liters of gasoline, I could not reasonably attempt to get to my son and my house.

Abel knows that the *Kommandanturs* granted some refugees five or ten liters of gas and that in Chapelon the ordnance trucks and the field kitchen had abundant supplies of it. He asks the corporal whether some couldn't be obtained by speaking to the lieutenant. But the corporal replies, "*Offizier . . . schlimm** . . ." And he pulls himself up to his full, enormous height, raises a finger level with his nose and repeats several times with an air of jubilation and pride, a sort of giddiness that only men with the lifesaving instincts of a Newfoundland know, "*Ich . . . Ich . . . Ich . . .*"

He will bring, he says, thirty liters of gasoline to us at the woodshed behind the farmhouse this very evening. But he asks that we wait until it is completely dark. The German word *Finsternis*† seems to have an incomparable poetry for me. *Finsternis* translates into sound the zigzag of lightning in the night. *Finsternis* contains the oft-invoked grace of darkness. *Finsternis* is the beautiful darkness crossed by a pale glow that guides the corporal from the reaches of the orchard to the farm's woodshed.

A finger on his lips, the corporal also asks us not to say anything to the women. I promised, I swore: now I'm breaking my promise.

Around ten o'clock, I'm waiting with Abel in the woodshed. The corporal appears carrying a twenty-liter gas can, a gas can from an ordnance truck. Without giving us time to say a word, he puts it on the ground, signals us to hide the light and asks for a sack to conceal three five-liter cans he has yet to bring us.

The three of us are sitting at Abel Delaveau's table with a bottle of Savigny he fetched from his cellar. We're attempting a very strange conversation in which Abel and I are trying to explain to the colossal corporal the difference between Burgundies and bistro wines.

That is when I searched the furthest reaches of my German vocabulary. "I am not attempting," I tell him, "to remunerate you for your heart's good intentions or even your kindness. Those are not things one pays for. But I would at least like to reimburse you for the price of the gasoline."

It would have been easy for the colossal corporal to let me believe he had bought it or at least had "slipped a coin" to the truck driver. But he burst into laughter, the same laughter as a French soldier had he been asked how much he paid for patience or the polishing brush

* Officer . . . bad.
† Darkness.

he filched in the barracks to get ready for an inspection. His eyes were sparkling with satisfaction. That is how the colossal corporal, eight years into a twelve-year reenlistment, had run the risk, the most selfless of risks, to steal thirty-five liters of gasoline from Hitler and bring them to me.

I asked for his address in Germany. I planned to send him a cask of Beaujolais after the war. Would I ever be able to?

But I already felt the awakening, like the restlessness in one's legs during insomnia, of a shared nervous system between the car and myself; I was already anticipating the road, the trees flying by.

The following morning we leave Chapelon. Abel, like me, had seen the defeat. But from a distance we can hardly distinguish its consequences. We're blinded by the word *armistice*, which sounds provisional. I am leaving with the illusion that I'll see him again soon.

We roll along without a hitch. Toucy, Clamecy, Château-Chinon, Autun. We're crossing a landscape of automobiles, sidecars and wrecked motorcycles. The fields bordering the road are enclosed behind wrecked cars. But I see only Tournus and Saint-Amour at the end of the road, a Tournus and Saint-Amour outside the space and time of the war, a Tournus and Saint-Amour outside space and time, a Tournus and Saint-Amour that are ours alone and only within us.

Having been wandering nomads and stationary nomads, we're sensitized, as they say in laboratory terms, to familiar landscapes. The ship's apprentice in maritime stories who cries "Land!" from the masthead, I understand the joy of his cry. The clean lines of the Yonne countryside, the tall curtains of trees, the strong contours of the land, the river without flourishes or embellishments, we recover them as if they had been stolen.

Outside Toucy, I don't recall where, we stop to eat a few hard-boiled eggs. There had been fighting there, or troops had been harried by aircraft. Shirts, empty bottles, shoes, a pair of bloody pants. Letters, those pitiful letters, are strewn in the roadside ditch. This heap of debris stretches as far as the eye can follow the ditch.

The roads are lined with woods, winding uphill and down. Château-Chinon appears, like a fortress built in the trees, hanging from the sky. We pass through villages with bombed-out houses. We pass German convoys and motorcyclists. As we approach Chalon, I can't say whether the countryside is beautiful. Too many memories are attached to it. It is flat, rolling, of a slightly soft material. The eye sinks into it.

We go into a grocery store. The young grocer has the look of tender nonchalance that many women in the region have. Her r's are perfectly rolled, polished, frictionless, bathed in oil. The Saône has this accent when it's not acting like an Indochinese river near Fleurville.

I stayed in Chalon only a few minutes. But there I saw a moon man. His round face was that of a real man, an average man. He was resting his elbows on his windowsill, watching the road benevolently. I don't know what information I asked him for, but he responded as if there had been no war, as if the Germans weren't in Chalon, as if it were still July 1939.

"Oh, come on," I said to him, "it looks like Chalon is occupied to me . . ."

He answered in a faraway voice, eyes wide, "Yes . . . Personally, I saw a few German soldiers . . . But we lack for nothing . . ."

Don't go looking for an indication of the Chalonnais soul here. But I would have liked to find out whether the man had really fallen from the moon or was crazy.

We cross Chalon, arriving at the border between the occupied zone and the free zone . . . An officer or noncommissioned officer with the face of a pedantic jurist examines our papers. We can cross, but he informs us that we will no longer be able to reenter the occupied zone. Indeed, a long line of cars headed in the opposite direction is not moving. We feel pity for these homeless, but quickly we are no more than sixty kilometers from home.

We're now driving in the free zone. We never imagined we could be so taken by a word. Free, we're free. Free in France. The words make us giddy. The land is no longer covered with Germans; the land is no longer covered with defeat. We can go where we like, forward, backward, right as easily as left. We were living half asphyxiated. We are entering an aerated world. Customs are easygoing and subtler than rules. The air that enters our chests is lighter. It's the air of freedom; at least we think so. It makes us giddy. We're no longer used to it. Poor Abel Delaveau in your farmhouse where the noncoms use your table.

What happens tomorrow isn't important for the moment. We're not calculating how much of France is under the boot and how much isn't. The armistice is nothing but a pause, an interlude that allows a person to recompose himself. We're not thinking in terms of history but rather in terms of our route, each of whose curves I know. Like one remembers his childhood in an old house, I recover everything that, in my life, was hope and love.

The road is narrow, bordered with hedges. It's no national highway, but a road all the same. An old woman sitting on a campstool is there watching over her three goats. She has set up her stool half on the grass median and half on the edge of the roadway. Her goats wander from one hedge to the other. If I tried to pass, I'd crush either a goat or the old woman. Before the war, before the German occupation, I'd no doubt have allowed myself some fit of rage. At least I'd have cursed that old woman, who dared disrupt the ideal line of my route, who dared disrupt my schedule. Dear old woman, I now know that French roads are made for old women and goats, too. Dear old woman whose campstool was jutting into the road, I nearly got out of the car to kiss you.

An hour later, we arrived. We had left Paris June 11th. It was July 13th. I got back my son and the peace of familiar fields, land and sky. And newspapers, too, and human error and what must be called history. But history and newspapers, that's another story.

THE NEVERSINK LIBRARY

THE NEVERSINK LIBRARY

THE NEVERSINK LIBRARY

DEFINITELY MAYBE
by Arkady and Boris Strugatsky

978-1-61219-281-9
$15.00 / $15.00 CAN

GILGI
by Irmgard Keun

978-1-61219-277-2
$16.00 / $16.00 CAN

THE GRAVEYARD
by Marek Hłasko

978-1-61219-294-9
$15.95 / $15.95 CAN

REASONS OF STATE
by Alejo Carpentier

978-1-61219-279-6
$16.95 / $16.95 CAN

ZULEIKA DOBSON
by Max Beerbohm

978-1-61219-292-5
$15.95 / $15.95 CAN

LEAVETAKING
by Peter Weiss

978-1-61219-331-1
$16.00 / $16.00 CAN

INSEL
by Mina Loy

978-1-61219-353-3
$15.00 / $15.00 CAN

**LETTERS OF JAMES AGEE
TO FATHER FLYE**

978-1-61219-361-8
$16.00 / $16.00 CAN

SPECIMEN DAYS AND COLLECT
by Walt Whitman

978-1-61219-386-1
$15.95 / $15.95 CAN

TIRRA LIRRA BY THE RIVER
by Jessica Anderson

978-1-61219-388-5
$15.95 / $15.95 CAN

33 DAYS
by Léon Werth

978-1-61219-425-7
$16.00 / $16.00 CAN

THE DEAD MOUNTAINEER'S INN
by Arkady and Boris Strugatsky

978-1-61219-433-2
$17.00 / $17.00 CAN